INTERNET FOR CATS

INTERNET
FOR CATS

Judy Heim

no starch press

Publisher: William Pollock

Cover and Interior Illustrator: Alan Okamoto

Cover and Interior Designer: Cloyce Wall

Dummier & Compositor: Steven Bolinger

Copyeditor: Deborah Gravitz

Proofreader: Carol Lombardi

Printed in Canada

1 2 3 4 5 6 7 8 9 10—99 98 97 96

Distributed to the book trade in the United States and Canada by Publishers Group West, 4065 Hollis, P.O. Box 8843, Emeryville, California 94662, phone: 800-788-3123 or 510-548-4393, fax: 510-658-1834.

For information on translations or book distributors outside the United States, please contact No Starch Press directly:

No Starch Press,1903 Jameston Lane, Daly City, CA 94014-3466, phone: 415-334-7200, fax: 415-334-3166, CIS: 74012,2506, Internet: nostarch@ix.netcom.com.

Library of Congress Cataloging-in-Publication Data
Heim, Judy.
    Internet for cats / by Judy Heim.
       p.   cm.
    ISBN 1-886411-07-7
    1. Cats—Humor. 2. Internet (Computer network)—Humor.
    I. Title.
M6231.C23H45   1995   95-33732
025.06'6368—dc20

For Grendel, best cat ever

CONTENTS

Chapter Seven

Finding Smart Vets and Practical Medical Advice in Cyberspace 145

Chapter Eight

Internet Cat FAQ Goddesses Offer Advice on Love, Life, Cat Toys, and How to Live with a Human Without Going Insane 163

PREFACE

Because I'm primarily a publisher of computer books, I'm constantly dogged by would-be authors peddling Internet books. I can't pick up the phone without hearing frenetic pitches for yet another online book for dummies, wimps, or complete idiots. Last year, the publishing industry churned out 10,532 books about the Internet, which makes me wonder how there can be any dummies, wimps, or idiots still out there.

Last fall, I began receiving e-mail from an aspiring author named B. Rodilardus. He had some unique ideas for an Internet book that he wanted to write. For starters, he felt that the Internet had too many people on it. He thought that increased animal participation would improve the Net tremendously. He also believed that it was possible to communicate with FTP servers via something he called cat ESP. He proceeded to detail the process in a series of lengthy e-mail messages that at the time struck me, naive publisher that I was, as highly disturbed.

I ignored the messages, but they continued. Eventually I realized that the writer was not a crackpot. He was a cat.

That's how this book began.

WHY CATS LIKE THE INTERNET

The explosion of user-friendly interfaces and the proliferation of e-mail addresses that you can write to for free samples of cat food have made the Internet more popular than ever among cats. Its many avenues resembling endlessly branching, steamy alleys have lured thousands of cats to slink down and explore the mysterious darkness late into the night. Cat home pages on the World Wide Web have sprung up by the hundreds in all corners of the Internet, in countries as far-flung as the Netherlands and Japan. There are Internet discussion groups for cats, mailing lists for cats, "frequently asked question" files for cats, even gopher servers for cats.

If you've ever spotted Fluffy sitting on your keyboard, staring wide-eyed at the screen or batting the mouse around the desk, you know that cats have an enduring interest in computers. No other appliance since the electric can opener has fascinated cats to such a degree. Left alone with a computer, most cats will claim it as their own and proceed to reprogram macros, gnaw on disk drive doors, and drop hair into every open vent. Cats are born Net cruisers; their willingness to sit in the same spot for hours without blinking, coupled with their ability to maintain their cool around computers (unless they fall off one), gives them distinct advantages over other mammals when it comes to prowling the information highway.

BUBBLES RODILARDUS VANISHES

After much thought, I concluded that the world was in need of a good Internet guide for cats. I decided to pay B. Rodilardus, or Bubbles, as I came to know him, a hefty advance to write one. As so often happens with computer-book authors, Bubbles wrote only the first chapter and half of an appendix, then absconded with the advance. He is rumored to have run off with a Net-surfing kitten he met on Mr. Puddy the Cat's home page. When we tried to call him, we found that his cellular phone had been turned off forever.

It was left to me to piece together the rest of the manuscript in time to meet the bookstore advance orders. From Bubbles's original e-mail messages, his wide-ranging dissertations on the uses of cat ESP on FTP servers, and fragments of text tucked between the gibberish left by his paws as he walked across the keyboard ("..iqwlalseipala.slllllllle.e.sei..."), I built a book that is as true to Bubbles's original intent as I could make it.

I won't apologize for Bubbles's trenchant dismissal of the Usenet newsgroup rec.pets.cats as a place "cluttered with canary-brained people who bulk-e-mail with bonehead theories about why their cats lick walls, as if there were anything wrong with that." Nor will I apologize for the book's provocative endorsement of flame mail, or its censure of vet schools that link their gopher servers to Harvard Medical School's computers, "which everyone knows suffers credibility problems since it lacks a cat teaching-hospital." These were Bubbles's deeply felt convictions.

Please don't write off Bubbles as a whiner; there are many features of the Internet that he enjoyed immensely and wanted to recommend to other cats, like the World Wide Web pages that cats call home, the pleasures of exchanging e-mail with other felines, and electronic shopping malls with pet-food stores. He also wanted to teach other cats how to walk properly on the keyboard and what to consider before their humans go shopping for computers.

More than anything, Bubbles wanted to see more cats on the Internet. Bubbles told us that for a cat, life on the Internet was like "a drawer full of elastic stockings—no matter where you poke, you discover something interesting to chew." This book, then, is Bubbles's guide for cats who want to cruise the Internet and make it their own.

WILLIAM POLLOCK
Publisher
No Starch Press

INTERNET FOR CATS

Part One

Internet for

Cool Cats

Chapter One

HOW TO BE A
NET SURFER IF
YOU'RE A CAT

My name is Bubbles. And like many cats, I was reluctant to prance down the information highway for the first time. I worried that I'd type something wrong and be mistaken for a poodle with a learning disability—or worse, a human. Convinced that every ground squirrel with a TRS-80 computer knew more about the Internet than I did, I preferred staying inside my circus tent-shaped cat bed, listening to *The Fur Person* on tape for the umpteenth time rather than taking a seat on the computer keyboard.

My fears were groundless. I soon discovered that I didn't need to know anything about the Internet or computers to be a cybercat. All I had to do was log on, and my native gifts of feline charm, social genius, and knavish wit would carry me as far down the infobahn as my four impeccably pedicured paws wished to range. It wasn't long before my address book swelled with the e-mail addresses of cat-babes lounging on keyboards around the globe.

Oh yes, there were occasional starlings who dared call me a newbie (you'll find their feathers stored in a gopher server in Sri Lanka). There were also rubes who questioned my right to bombard every computer user on the Internet with e-mail decrying the labeling practices of certain cat-food companies (you know the ploy—they call something "meaty parts," but it's rarely the meaty parts that you'd expect). The ninnies called my mass-mailing a *spam*, a gross breach of Internet etiquette they said, and their whining got me thrown off the Internet—but not for long. I was soon back online with a new password.

So as you surf the Net, remember: You, not the gutless gopher-brains who crowd cyberspace, are the creature of beauty and intelligence. You, not the ignorant rabble who compose endless messages about why cats eat cellophane tape, are a direct descendant of the Egyptian cat goddess Bastet (you also probably have a more colorful collection of cat bowls than they do). You, not that easily confused hunk of plastic called a computer, have been the subject of songs, poems, and tapestries for thousands of years. The computer has been the subject of a few posters and an online diatribe or two, but that's about it.

In short, keep in mind that you are the superior being—superior to computers, superior to people, superior to anyone and anything you encounter on the electronic highway. You are even superior to the Internet itself. As long as you remember this, you will become a cybercat in no time.

To get started, you will need to assemble these powerful Internet tools:

- A computer and accessories mighty enough to reflect your leonine powers

- An Internet link, preferably one that works with cat ESP

- A human willing and able to install your Internet software, plug your modem into the telephone jack, clean up your e-mail subdirectories, and serve as your love slave

- A stick with a feather on the end that you can play with when you tire of the Internet and the idiots who clog it

I'll teach you how to get these Internet tools working shortly.

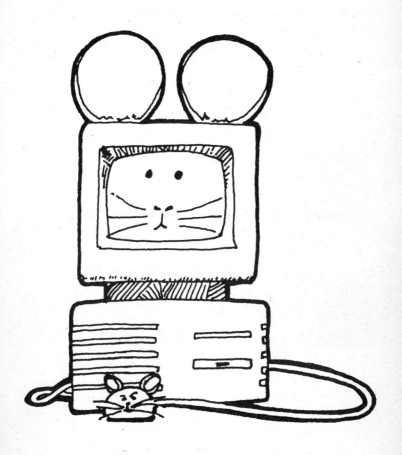

COMPUTERS ARE NOTHING BUT BIG CAT TOYS

Computers are the ultimate playthings for higher forms of intelligent life (meaning cats, not the mutt under the desk and the human pimple in sneakers who dragged him home). Stick a paw into the computer's tape-drive door to hear the satisfying whir of the tape reader contacting fur instead of magnetic tape. Hop onto the keys and listen to the beep-beep of startled microchips fearful that they're about to become a snack in a whiskered mouth. Bat the mouse from its perch and watch it hang inertly in the air, like subdued prey in an archetypal cat dream.

Unfortunately, most humans buy a computer with a muddled sense of purpose. They think they're buying the computer for themselves. They think they're buying it to get work done. Their minds are so clouded that they forget what a computer really is: a giant cat toy. Before your human starts shopping, you must distract her from her preoccupation with bus speeds and hard disk capacities and remind her to buy you the kind of computer that you will need to stay ahead in today's global information society. Rub against her ankles and use your cat ESP to tell her to shop for these things:

A mini-tower computer. It's easier to glue shag carpet to the sides of a mini-tower than to a desktop case. And it's more fun to push things over the edge of a mini-tower.

A monitor that's at least 17 inches wide. Nothing's more insulting than listening to the complaints of a human seated behind you who's tired of craning his neck to get a glimpse of the screen.

A mouse with a very long cord. Make sure it has one of those rubber balls in it so that you can pry it out and bat it around when you're bored.

A printer with ample seating area. You want one that gets warm so that you'll be less apt to catch a draft from the computer's fan while you're napping.

Make sure that your human doesn't buy any of these:

A plastic keyboard cover to keep your hair from falling between the keys and shorting out the keyboard. They're as degrading as couches covered by plastic slipcovers.

Multimedia CD-ROM encyclopedias with dogs barking. The last thing you want is to become startled and fall off the desk while you're exchanging e-mail with Bill Gates.

Cat Net Surfer Tip

Like life itself, computing is often best enjoyed while sitting in a warm lap.

WHAT KIND OF INTERNET LINK IS BEST FOR CATS?

When it's time to connect to the Internet, ignore the technotalk about SLIP/PPP connections, high-speed T1 connections, and other such nonsense. All you need is an Internet link that will work with cat ESP. Cat ESP is what you use when you sit motionless in front of the refrigerator, thinking hard, and suddenly the door pops open.

Cat ESP works on the Internet, too. Unlike humans, you don't have to read any of those 1,500-page Internet encyclopedias. Nor will you need to sign up for those $3,000 seminars that teach you how to distinguish your e-mail address from the number on your rabies vaccination tag. All you need to do is stare hard at the computer screen. When confronted by cat ESP, even the Internet will do your bidding.

You can you tell whether an Internet service works with cat ESP by sitting on its magazine advertisement. If you sit on a computer magazine long enough, the Internet will communicate to you telepathically through the fur on your back whether or not the service supports cat ESP.

If your cat ESP somehow deserts you, don't despair. You can still log on to the Internet and navigate it with ease. Just have your human call CompuServe, Prodigy, or America Online and ask for a free startup kit. You can tap into the Internet from any of those services.

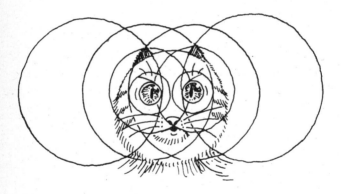

Training a Human to Serve as Your Internet Slave

Once your human has set up the computer, you must convince her to turn it over to you. Start by circling her chair with your tail high in the air. When she glances down, meow pitifully like a tiny kitty. When she invites you onto her lap, hop up and rub up against her. Purr and squeeze your eyes together like you mean business and stroke your whiskers against her hand to beg for more. Let her scratch your chin.

The minute she's distracted, make a flying leap at the keyboard.

Your first keyboard landing will probably be clumsy. If you're lucky, the computer will beep. If you're especially lucky, you may activate a spread-sheet-reformatting menu. More likely than not, your future Internet slave will snatch you from the keyboard and toss you to the floor.

Don't be discouraged. Hop back up immediately, but this time scamper over the keys, walking over as many as possible.

When your human deposits you back on the floor, jump on the keyboard yet again. This time plant your behind on the home row, bat at the computer screen, and scream bloody murder if she tries to remove you.

While it may take days for the household computer expert to become your Internet slave, she'll eventually abandon it to you. She'll realize that the computer was always yours and that your purposes for it are far loftier than hers.

Cat Net Surfer Tip

To sign up for America Online, call 800-827-6364 or write to America Online, 8619 Westwood Center Dr., Vienna, VA 22182 and ask for the free startup kit to receive the software you need to open an account (specify Windows, DOS, or Macintosh). You can buy the CompuServe start-up kit in stores or get it free from CompuServe. Call CompuServe at 800-848-8199 or 614-457-8600 or write to the company at 5000 Arlington Centre Blvd., Columbus, OH 43220. You'll receive one of the CompuServe Information Manager programs (for either Windows, DOS, or Macintosh) and a free trial offer.

If you contact these services yourself, don't tell them you're a cat; they may not accept your credit card.

Before you can cruise the Internet, you must learn to use the keyboard. Follow this guide to walking properly:

Basic Keyboard Walking

Many of us make the mistake of trampling the keyboard too quickly. Learn to prance gracefully, feel the squish of the keys beneath your toes, and circle the keyboard (pretend you're patrolling the periphery of a garden). Rub your chin against the monitor to mark it with your scent. Don't worry if a little cat hair falls between the keys—if you short out the keyboard your human can always buy you a new one.

Keyboard Properly

Advanced Keyboard Walking

Once you've mastered basic keyboard walking, try some advanced tricks. A note of warning to cats with Garfield-esque physiques: When you jump on the keyboard, if the computer beeps as shrilly as if a watermelon had fallen on it, stick to traversing the keys slowly until your veterinarian approves the more strenuous workouts below.

The Household Kamikaze Shoot out from behind the computer and pounce on the keyboard. Land with all four feet straddling the keys. When your human tries to remove you, grasp the keys with your claws and scream. The keyboard will come flying after you.

The Playful Predator Sneak Attack with Mouse Ambush When your Internet slave is absorbed in his work, sneak up behind his chair. Surprise him by flying up onto the desk and scurrying across the keyboard. Rattle as many keys as you can. When your human springs up to nab you, leap over the printer, knocking the mouse to the floor. Hightail it out of the room.

The Earring Bat-and-Pounce Assault From a concealed position, leap onto the lap of the human hunched in front of the computer. Reach up and bat her dangling earrings. While her hands are busy protecting her ears, hop onto the keyboard and plant your behind on the Scroll key. Do not budge until the screen goes black.

Power User Tip for Alley Cats
BEFRIENDING A STRAY COMPUTER GEEK

You've been living on the street for most of your life, relatively happy, foraging through trash cans, fighting in alleys. But you yearn for more. You want to get on the info highway and make a name for yourself, maybe link up with a high-profile cattery or pick up some cyber-cat babes. Street life won't give you access to a 125 MHz Pentium with 30 megs of RAM and a graphics accelerator card, so you need to find a stray computer geek to move in with.

Now we know that any human who gets down on his hands and knees on a busy city sidewalk to cry "Kitty! Kitty!" is more than likely to provide you with the coddled life that you seek. But how do you know if he has a computer? Easy. When he chases you down the alley, if he pants hard, doubles over, grabs his chest, and gasps, "Migod, I … haven't … run this far … since the … sack race … at the Microsoft … company barbecue!" he probably owns a computer. If all the pens fall out of his shirt pocket when he coughs, it's a sure thing. Move in for the kill.

Cat Net Surfer Tip

Don't worry if the computer is advertised as having a "small footprint." That doesn't mean it can walk, at least not very far.

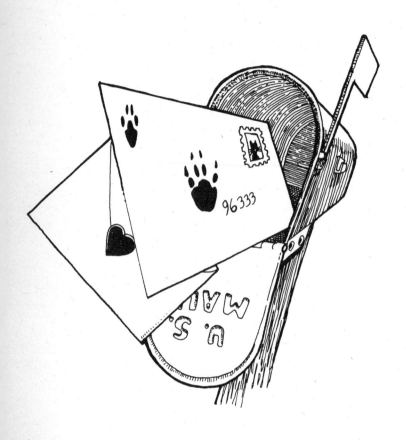

Chapter Two

CATS WHO SEND

E-MAIL

Humans tend to regard e-mail as a clumsy medium, in which shy maidens are mistaken for frothing ogres and a harmless jest is easily misconstrued as an angry barb. We cats, on the other hand, consider e-mail the ideal vehicle for communicating our genius. It lets us translate our subtle gestures and body language perfectly into pithy missives full of exclamation points, childish emotions, catcalls, and the piercing insults of which e-mail flame wars are made.

E-mail is simply a message that you tap out on your computer and send, over phone lines or a computer network like the Internet, to another computer to be read by a creature who is invariably less important than you are. On the surface, your e-mail may bubble with fond reminiscences of toys, rodents, or sunny gardens. But beneath its innocent veneer, the recipient should see that you are far more intelligent, interesting, and significant than he could ever hope to be.

PROFILE OF A FELINE
E-MAIL EXCHANGE

Here is an example of a cat e-mail exchange that I ran across recently in an area of the Internet occupied by Persian cats discussing the difficulty of keeping their tails from catching fire during motherboard upgrades. It began with a friendly note from a cat named Frank residing at the Cattery (an institution of higher education). He wrote it to a cat named Peony whose glamour photo he spotted on the World Wide Web. The correspondence went like this.

TO: peony@feline.com
FROM: frank@cattery.edu

Dear Ms. Peony,
I discovered your e-mail address and picture on Mr. Puddy's World Wide Web home page. I don't think I've ever seen such a silky cat. Or one with such big yellow eyes. I enjoy sleeping on a Naugahyde chair all day. I know how to pry open dorm-sized mini-fridges with one paw. I once had to be rushed to the animal hospital for eating a glow-in-the-dark spider that came from a cereal box. That's about the sum of me. Now tell me about you.
Sincerely,
Frank the Maine Coon Cat

TO: frank@cattery.edu
FROM: peony@feline.com

Dearest Frank,
Prrrrrr! You sound like a cat of many talents. I bet you're big and strong and can scare a rottweiler up a tree. Prrrrrrrr! <curling fluffy body around> I don't think I've ever seen a dorm fridge. I eat my dinner out of a cut-crystal bowl. My hobbies include lying on satin, lying on floral chintz, lying on hand-painted silk, and sitting on brocade (I don't like to lie on brocade because it makes my fur crinkle in funny directions). Prrrrr!
Love,
Peony <blinking demurely>

TO: peony@feline.com
FROM: frank@cattery.edu

Dear Ms. Peony,
Boy, we have a lot in common! I have a dinner bowl, too, but I don't eat out of it. I'd rather chew the cat food into tiny pieces, spit them out onto the linoleum, and eat it that way. I've never seen a rottweiler, but I was once chased through a ditch by a mole. It was a big one, too. Do you like to climb around water-treatment facilities at night?
Sincerely,
Frank the Maine Coon Cat

TO: frank@cattery.edu
FROM: peony@feline.com

Dearest Adorable Frank,
I prefer to spend my nights sitting on the windowsill waiting for luscious tomcats like you to appear out of the darkness. Prrrrrr! <tail swishing>
Love,
Peony

TO: peony@feline.com
FROM: frank@cattery.edu

Dear Ms. Peony,
Yow! No one's ever said that to me before—at least not on the Internet. I would love to hear you purr in person. I have a big-screen TV that we could both sit on together. Do you like Hartz Mountain Bizzy-Balls? I have some of those, too. Yow!
Sincerely,
Frank the Maine Coon Cat

TO: frank@cattery.edu
FROM: peony@feline.com

My Virile Frank,
Prrrrrrrrrrrrrrrrrrr! I bet you're beautiful when you sing to a woman in the moonlight. Do you know how to sing Strauss's "Tanz der Sieben Schleier"? Nothing excites me so much as hearing "Tanz der Sieben Schleier," particularly the Philadelphia Orchestra/Eugene Ormandy version. Prrrrrrrrrrr!
<blinking eyes expectantly>
Peony
P.S. I only sit on the TV during *Masterpiece Theatre*.

TO: *peony@feline.com*
FROM: *frank@cattery.edu*

Dear Ms. Peony,
How 'bout the Beach Boys' "Surfin' Safari"? I could sing that to you.
Sincerely,
Frank the Maine Coon Cat

TO: frank@cattery.edu
FROM: peony@feline.com

My Dear Jesting Frank,
Perhaps you know instead Prokofiev's "Suite from the Love for Three Oranges"? Here, I'll start you out on the first note: Yeeoowww!
<eyes closing in rapture>
Peony

TO: peony@feline.com
FROM: frank@cattery.edu

Dear Ms. Peony,
Are you sure you wouldn't prefer the Beach Boys' "I Get Around"?
Sincerely,
Frank the Maine Coon Cat
P.S. Wasn't Prokofiev a drummer for George Michael?

When Frank the Maine Coon Cat did not hear from Ms. Peony for over a week, he wrote to her again, this time including in the message the lyrics from the Beach Boys' "I Get Around." He included all the "round, rounds."

Peony's response was not what Frank had hoped. Her message was full of Hsssssssses and Phffffts, ppppppppppppppppppeeeeeeeeeeeeeeeeeeees, and Get outa my sight, you mangy tomcat, before I rip your whiskers off and bite your tails, as well as other signs that she had paced angrily back and forth over the keyboard. It was clear to poor Frank that Ms. Peony was no longer in heat.

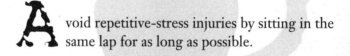

Cat Net Surfer Tip

Avoid repetitive-stress injuries by sitting in the same lap for as long as possible.

THE UNSPOKEN RULES OF CAT E-MAIL

You may have noticed several principles of cat etiquette at work in the above e-mail exchange. To begin with, both participants refrained from threatening to pull out the other's whiskers until the very end of the correspondence. Furthermore, since the Internet is not set up so that new acquaintances can sit and merely stare at each other for an interminable length of time, Ms. Peony improvised by suggesting body postures. Cats do this with triangular brackets, as in <curling fluffy body around>. Cat sounds also translate very well into e-mail, as in *Hsss!* and *Pffftt!* Until more cats acquire voice modems that allow you to communicate with simultaneous voice and text, *meow* is usually spelled out.

Another guideline for polite creatures: One correspondent does not barrage the other with multiple e-mail messages without waiting for a response. For instance, you write another cat, who writes you back, and so on. This antiphony is similar to the overture to a cat fight—you hiss, they hiss back—but infinitely more refined.

Finally, an e-mail correspondent threatens to bite off the reader's tail only in extreme situations, like when he says you have the TCP/IP stack of a sissy. These other rules of feline netiquette apply in cyberspace as well:

Rules of Feline
E-mail Deportment

Cat Net Surfer Rule #1: *Never answer an e-mail message unless you know what's in it for you.*

This is the only way to ensure that your e-mail box is not flooded with childish messages from people whining about their broken computers or dysfunctional offices, or worse, their misbehaving cats. This way you receive only important communiqués from other cats, like messages describing bowls of goldfish, pictures knocked on floors, and the art of hiding upside-down in ripped couches.

Cat Net Surfer Rule #2: *It's OK to ask dumb questions on the Internet, so long as your audience knows that you're vastly superior to them.*

Note Frank's question to Peony in the earlier exchange: "Do you like to climb around water-treatment facilities at night?" Of course every cat does. But Frank had no compunction about asking this dumb question because he knows that when you're a technosavvy cat you're superior to everyone.

Cat Net Surfer Rule #3: *You can use special cat emoticons to express your cat emotions, but…*

When you start writing e-mail messages, you may find it difficult to convey all nuances of your cat emotions (the arched back, the wide eyes, the bared teeth). Fluffing your fur to look dangerous works great when other cats are around, but when you do it in front of the computer screen no one can see you.

What's more, many complex layers underlie cat emotions, and they're hard to express in e-mail. For instance, when you start writing the message you might feel peevish. Halfway through you find yourself in a good mood, a few sentences later you're depressed, and by the end of the message you're feeling peevish again. How do you express all these states of mind in your e-mail? You can try something cute, like inserting little pictures called *emoticons* into your e-mail. Here are some of the most expressive:

Cat Emoticons

```
 ^ ^
 o o
 =*=
```

Staring at you.

```
 ^ ^
 O O
 =*=
```

Night vision in operation.

```
 ^ ^
 - -
 =*=
```

My eyes may be closed, but my mind
is hatching new mischief.

```
 ^ ^
 * *
 =*=
  U
```

Acckk!

```
^   ^
O   O
=*=    Hssss!
 \/
```

Eager to terrorize basset hound on
World Wide Web dog page.

```
^   ^
O   O
=*=
^^  ^^
```

Claws need pruning, keep sticking to
programmer's "prayer stool."

```
^   ^
X   X
=+=
 U
```

About to spit up hairball
on numeric keypad.

Everything here is mine.

You may be from another planet,
but I am too and I got here first.

```
  ^   ^

  .   O

  =O=

   ~ ~
```

If I weren't stuck in this apartment, I
would be a powerful world leader, and I'd
get to wear a monocle, too.

How to Start a Flame War

When coy pictures just don't cut it, try a more aggressive tactic: Ignite a flame war. This is my battle code:

Flame War Rule #1: *When you're really mad, spark a flame war.*

A flame war is the electronic equivalent of a hissy fit. You push someone, they push you back. Suddenly you're both rolling on the floor, kicking, clawing, and yowling. It's almost as much fun as body-slamming a shar pei.

My favorite warmongering technique: I head to a discussion group packed with lots of duck-stupid humans. I post a message like "Anyone who doesn't believe that most UFOs are sent here by cats from outer space should be entered in the Big and Stupid category at the Westminster Dog Show." The idea is to insult as many types of humans and animals in as short a message as possible. As you can see, this message insults: (1) UFO believers, (2) UFO skeptics, (3) UFOs, (4) cats from outer space, (5) big, stupid creatures, (6) dogs, (7) members of the Westminster Kennel Club, and (8) New Yorkers. This covers 99.999 percent of the regulars on the Internet. Don't worry about the rest; they're probably busy trying to fish their plastic pocket protectors out of their cat litter boxes.

Another good way to start a flame war is to head to one of the cat-related discussion groups and fire off a message that says "Clumping cat litter causes [insert name of favorite cat disease]." This never fails to get the fur flying. Within hours you'll have a flame war that stretches from rec.pets.cats into rec.pets.dogs and includes all the above-mentioned UFO believers, UFO skeptics, cats from outer space, New Yorkers, and so on. The dust won't settle for days. That's because Internet habitués take their brands of cat litter very seriously.

Flame War Rule #2: *One of the best things about the Internet is that when you get mad, no one can throw a blanket on you and drag you into the house.*

Never let a flame war reach a peaceable conclusion. That would defeat its purpose. Ideally, you want to get as many creatures as mad at each other as you can. That is the only way to expunge the anguish from your own delicate feline soul. Remember, on the Internet no one can bite your ear, pull your tail, or knock you off your cat tree. Should someone threaten to, just turn off your computer.

Cat Net Surfer Tip

M ost Internet flame wars are started by cats who did not get what they wanted for supper.

What's in a Cat's E-mail Address?

Three elements make up your Internet e-mail address: your computer name or log-on, the symbol @, and a suffix that designates the kind of computer service or network you use to receive your mail. For example, fluffy@feline.com is an Internet address for a cat named Fluffy at a research organization called Feline, Inc. Here are some suffixes you may spot at the end of cat e-mail addresses:

@grimalkin.org   A reform school for cats located under a hydrangea bush beneath the windows of the Armonk, New York office of IBM. (The *"org"* is short for *"organization"*; this is the Grimalkin Organization.) Grimalkin is one of Thomas Watson Sr.'s social projects of the '50s run amok. Every night thousands of cats run through the halls of IBM, shedding cat hair on all the computer keyboards. Rumor has it that this is the reason IBM lost ground to Apple in the computer wars. Executives are alleged to have cried, "Apples?! Who's got time to worry about Apples with all these cats running through the halls?"

@cattery.edu   This refers to an institution of higher learning (*edu* is short for *education*) known as the Cattery. The Cattery hosts cats who conduct scientific experiments ranging from wildly chasing their tails and carefully monitoring human responses to rolling on concrete and measuring the dirt that accumulates on their fur.

@chessycat.com   Formerly a railroad, Chessycat International is now an investment holding company (*com* designates a commercial entity). Run entirely by cats, Chessycat is allegedly responsible for the creation and proliferation of the risky investment device known as derivatives. Whenever investment managers shrug their shoulders and say, "I have no idea where the $48 trillion from the pension plan went," chances are that it went to Chessycat, where it was used to buy large numbers of sticks with feathers on the end.

@feline.com   Feline, Inc., is a worldwide commercial research effort dedicated to finding out how stupid humans really are. Formerly a joint venture of MIT and Xerox, Feline descended into madness in 1979 after a large tortoiseshell cat sat on an experimental fax-photocopy machine and faxed a photocopy of her behind to every scientific organization in the world.

@fidonet.org   Sure, this worldwide bulletin board system has a dog's name (*org* is short for *organization*). But that will change soon. Don't be surprised when Fidonet is renamed Catnet and the number of flame wars it hosts increases astronomically.

@whitehouse.gov   This is the office of Socks, Friskies-loving leader of the Western world and owner of a madcap family called the Clintons. (*Gov* designates government e-mail.)

@kilkennycat.mil   Conspiracy theorists believe that a secret government runs our nation's military. (*Mil* designates a military organization.) What they don't know is that this secret government, called Kilkenny, is made up of cats: very fat cats with silvery, suspicious eyes. They spend their days lying around, biting their claws, and sitting on the *New York Times* crossword puzzle while other government employees struggle to fill in the squares. They often work out of Socks's office. (See @white-house.gov.)

How to Tell If an E-mail Message Was Written by a Cat

Here are some easy ways to tell whether an e-mail message was written by a cat:

- 🐾 The writer wonders why, when you spring at a computer, it doesn't run off and hide in a window well.

- 🐾 The writer's e-mails are all missing the letter *C*. She explains that one night, while in a playful mood, she pried it off the keyboard and batted it under the desk.

- 🐾 The writer goes on to say that she occasionally likes to climb down from the computer chair and peer under the desk at the *C* key.

- 🐾 The writer asks if you've ever stuck your paw in the door of a tape-backup drive, just to feel around inside.

- 🐾 While discussing Windows 95, the writer asks if you've ever climbed drapes and hung from the valance rod by your toes.

- 🐾 The writer seems aloof, whiny, and vaguely superior. She makes you want to spring up and bat your paws at the screen.

- 🐾 The writer ends the message abruptly, explaining that she must run behind the computer to spit up a hairball.

CAN YOU KEEP OUT OF CATFIGHTS ON THE INFO HIGHWAY? AND IF SO, DO YOU WANT TO?

The Internet has a special code for online behavior. It's called *netiquette*. Netiquette requires that computer users behave nicely toward each other, refraining from such improprieties as cluttering up other users' mailboxes with unnecessary e-mail and making pigs of themselves by hogging precious network or computer resources. Of course, none of these rules apply to cats. We felines have our own special netiquette. It's based on the precept that we never pass up an opportunity to show others how important we are and that we don't take insults lightly. Here are some highlights:

If anyone calls you a newbie, fight back! Don't stand for being called the new kid on the block in Internet slang. Being a cat, you're street-wise no matter where you go. Tell the name-caller to GETALIFE! (type it in all caps for emphasis), then flash the emoticon for "I Once Clawed the Tail Off a Doberman Pinscher," thusly:

```
^  ^
O  O
=*=
^^   ^^    =======  <- dog tail 4 sale,
                       hardly used
```

Be careful when you tell people you're directly descended from the Egyptian cat goddess Bastet. The danger is, other cats will think you can help them solve their computer problems. You can, of course, but do you really want to? Let them solve their own problems.

Remember, you own the Internet. The Internet is yours and you should use it accordingly. Don't hesitate to log on to the computer of the University of Antwerp during the busiest time of the day to download five-megabyte pictures of glamour cats. So what if their computer crashes?

Know the emoticon for "I Have Claws," and use it. As in most real-life situations, diplomacy is useless on the Net. The only thing better than a big vocabulary of cutting insults is membership in a wild animal pack of other Internet denizens.

```
    ^   ^
    o   o
    =*=
   ^^   ^^
   ^^   ^^
```

Claws R Us

Join in when lots of people are arguing. Remember that you always have something important to say. Be sure to get your two cents in whenever you can, thus saving yourself the trouble of starting your own flame wars.

It's OK to play with people's minds. Granted, it's not clear that humans really have them, but if they think they do, play along. After all, what can they do to you when they discover that you're not really David Letterman tapping into the Rottie-L mailing list in search of performers for Stupid Human Tricks?

Chapter Three

CATS WITH WEB PAGES

One of the problems with the Internet is that people can't always see what a fine and beautiful cat you are. Many cats have found that the solution is to get their own World Wide Web page. A Web page is like an electronic billboard with your whiskers on it.

The World Wide Web is the part of the Internet that contains vid-game-like graphics, sounds, and video clips. You can tap into the Web from an Internet-only service like Netcom or any similar local service in your city. To view World Wide Web pages, you use either the service's Web-browsing software, like Netcruiser, or a Web-navigation program like Netscape or Mosaic. You can also tap into the World Wide Web through all the major online services including CompuServe, America Online, Prodigy, and the Microsoft Network, though you may need to download some special software to do so. Head to the service's main Internet menu for directions.

Hundreds of cats now have their own Web pages, where they display pictures of themselves, discuss their hobbies and obsessions, and impart their views on life and politics. Even Socks, the First Cat, has his own Web page (see page 63).

HOW TO WEB WALK IF YOU HAVE FOUR FEET

You get to the Web pages of other cats by typing into your Web browser the address for the page, for example
http://www.power.cats/smithey.html/
Type carefully; one wrong character, and you won't connect.

When you arrive at the page, a picture of a cat usually greets you. If you're lucky, it will be a good-looking cat, with wide, luminous eyes and a Cheshire grin. If you're unlucky, you might encounter the hideous face of a dog, in which case you should disconnect immediately.

If you like what you see on the Web page, you click on highlighted words or pictures, and you're whisked to other cat-related Web pages.

Cat Net Surfer Tip

Disk drives are great places to store small objects, especially if they're apt to run away.

PUTTING CLAWS INTO YOUR WEB PAGE

So now you're thinking, "Hey, I want a Web page too!" If your human won't give you one, tromp on the keyboard and meow pitifully until she relents. Don't be conned when your human whines that a Web page is hard to build, and that she doesn't know the first thing about HTML coding. She can take a night course. There are certain responsibilities that come with sharing one's home with a cat, and these days one of those happens to be giving any cat in the house his or her own Web page.

The next step is to sign up for an Internet service that lets you create your own page. There's probably an Internet service in your community that will let you have your own page for a few dollars a month beyond their monthly subscription fee.

What should you put on your page once you acquire one? A picture of yourself is de rigueur. Post one that makes you look as cool as possible (check out Mr. Puddy's home page to see what I mean). You might include pictures of your friends or list your hobbies, like sitting on the couch and knocking potted plants off windowsills. If your human is technically adept (amazingly, some are), she will build into your Web page links to the home pages of other cats on the information highway (highly desirable because that way other cats can find you and even leave you messages).

It is perfectly OK to include on your page complaints about your human and how he refuses to let you sleep on his face at night, or how, after you spend 20 minutes trying to coax him to the kitchen, he opens the fridge and feeds his own face first. Just remember that the more complaints you list, the less enthusiastic your human will be about paying the monthly Internet fee to maintain your page. To keep him happy, you might pay him a compliment or two, or even let him include his picture on the page. (Humans love it when you let them put their pictures on your home page; they feel cool by association.)

Note: I've got my own Web page. Check me out at **http://execpc.com/~judyheim/internet4cats. html**

The World Wide Web

Cat-a-Log

Mr. Puddy the Cat's Home Page is one of the hottest spots on the Internet, partly because of Mr. Puddy's cool sunglasses but also because of the page's hot-link to the Cat Treat of the Month Club and the fact that you can talk to Mr. Puddy himself through a speech synthesizer. Mr. Puddy, whose real name is Mukta Augustus, of Ann Arbor, Michigan (*mukta* is Sanskrit for *liberation from mental angst*), also includes on his page birthday photos and glamour shots of himself in sundry poses for the benefit of any cat-babes who happen to surf past. As if this weren't enough, he dispenses advice to lonelyhearts and unemployed graduate students who send him e-mail. Pay him a visit at

**http://www.sils.umich.edu/~nscherer/
     Mukta.html**

Basil

Basil's Home Page is a textbook example of Internet cat cool. In the photo at the top of the page, Basil displays his characteristic playboy jauntiness. Scroll down the page to read an account of his wild birthday bash. You can even view pictures of Basil's latest shindig (including hangovers) and his custom-smoked salmon. Scroll further down for pictures of Basil's pals. (Basil is one of the most popular partiers on the Net.) Tucked at the bottom of the page is a hypertext link to Socks's page at the White House (just click on the word *Socks* to jump there) as well as a personal meow-message from Socks that you can play through your computer's speaker—an Internet cat status item to be sure! Visit Basil by heading to

http://augustus.csscr.washington.edu/ personal.bigstar-mosaic/basil.html

T-cat

Gatso and Coo are two Japanese cats who maintain this venerable page in Japan called T-cat. Here you'll find a database of book titles and images of B. Kliban cats. You'll also find a map of all the major cat home pages around the world. Their human companion, Hiromi Saito, is quoted as saying she's "testing to breed a virtual cat—I'll explain later." Head to T-cat by typing into your Web walker

http://www.timis.ac.jp/Tcat/CatHome.html

Tap into the international cat-picture archives in Norway where you'll find hundreds of cheesecake photos of feline cuties. If you'd like your own photo included, scan it and save it in GIF or JPEG format, then e-mail it to **wikne@lynx.uio.no.** Visit the archives at

http://lynx.uio.no/jon/gif/cats

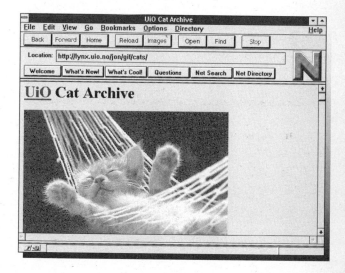

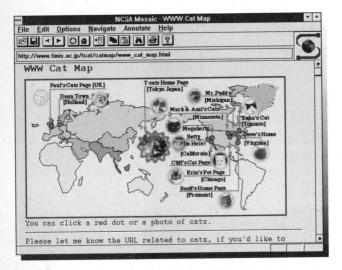

This global map of cat activity on the Web is a fix-
ture at the T-Cat site. It lists all the major cat home
pages, from the Pet Page in the United Kingdom,
to World Wide Cats in the Netherlands, to the two
spiritual hubs of cat culture on the Internet in
California and the Midwest. Click on any dot on
the map to go to the associated home page. You'll
find this map at

**http://www.timis.ac.jp/tcat/catmap/
www_cat_map.html**

Socks

It is a known fact that it is easiest to lead a world power while perched on the shoulder of a big guy wearing a baseball cap, as Socks, the First Feline, demonstrates on his Web page. To get there, head to the White House home page and click on Family Life. Be sure to click on the audio symbol to hear Socks meowing his opinions of Newt Gingrich. A textual translation is available: "Meow. Meow." Visit Socks at

http://www.whitehouse.gov

You know you've reached the pinnacle of info-
highway cool when your Web page is featured on
the World Wide Cats page in the Netherlands.
From here, you're just a mouse-click away from the
custom pages of dozens of other socially well connected cats around the globe. If you'd like your
photo included on World Wide Cats, scan it and e-
mail it as a GIF graphic file to **dmuller@xs4all.nl.**
Visit the World Wide Cats page at

http://news.xs4all.nl/~dmuller/wwc.html

The World Wide Cats Hall of Fame and the Cat of the Week are regular features on this page. When I last visited, the Cat of the Week was a luscious Norwegian forest cat named Snurran (*Prrrr*). You'll also find a hot-link to the Cat Fanciers' Home Page at

http://www.ai.mit.edu/fanciers/fanciers.html

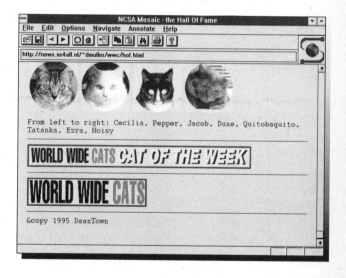

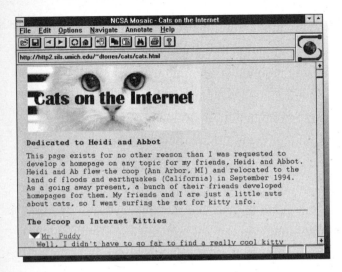

Leap from the Internet Cats Page into an online feline social whirl. You'll find links to dozens of cat home pages.

**http://http2.sils.umich.edu/~dtorres/cats/
cats.html**

For a change of paws, head to Darcy's page. Darcy is a 17-year-old, formerly homeless cat in New York City who was taken home by a cat lady. The page includes Darcy's reflections on history, politics, and his human's annoying habit of dressing him in costumes. In a high-tech audio meow portion you can hear his views on the most recent election. Classic! Visit Darcy at

http://www.intac.com:80/~kgs/darcy.html

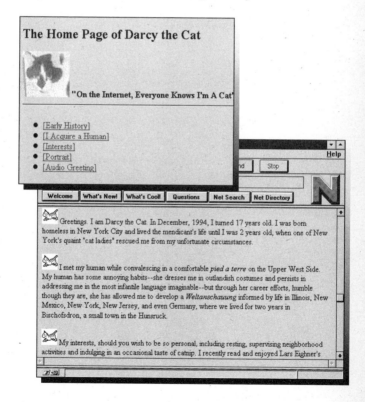

The Home Page of Darcy the Cat

"On the Internet, Everyone Knows I'm A Cat"

- [Early History]
- [I Acquire a Human]
- [Interests]
- [Portrait]
- [Audio Greeting]

Help

Stop

Welcome | What's New! | What's Cool! | Questions | Net Search | Net Directory

Greetings. I am Darcy the Cat. In December, 1994, I turned 17 years old. I was born homeless in New York City and lived the mendicant's life until I was 2 years old, when one of New York's quaint "cat ladies" rescued me from my unfortunate circumstances.

I met my human while convalescing in a comfortable *pied a terre* on the Upper West Side. My human has some annoying habits--she dresses me in outlandish costumes and persists in addressing me in the most infantile language imaginable--but through her career efforts, humble though they are, she has allowed me to develop a *Weltanschauung* informed by life in Illinois, New Mexico, New York, New Jersey, and even Germany, where we lived for two years in Bischofsdron, a small town in the Hunsruck.

My interests, should you wish to be so personal, including resting, supervising neighborhood activities and indulging in an occasional taste of catnip. I recently read and enjoyed Lars Eighner's

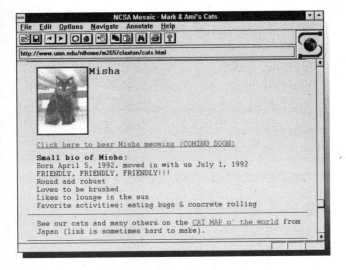

One advantage of being a black cat is that to look suave and brilliant, you need do nothing more than stand perfectly still. Misha is such a cat, and his page is little more than a fuzzy snapshot of himself and gushy notes from his human, but Misha's class shows through. His hobbies are eating bugs and rolling on concrete. Visit this debonair feline at

**http://www.umn.edu/nlhome/m265/claxton/
cats.html**

Pilate and Tatoosh give their page a homespun look by displaying family photos and letting their human write the copy. Tatoosh (or is it Pilate?) uses a laundry basket to good effect by standing in it. The two cavort in a blanket to show that their relationship is an open one. Visit them at

**http://www.umich.edu/~cambridg/
    CatPage.html**

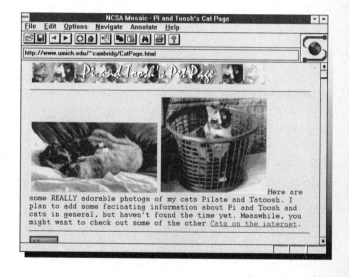

Talk to Cat

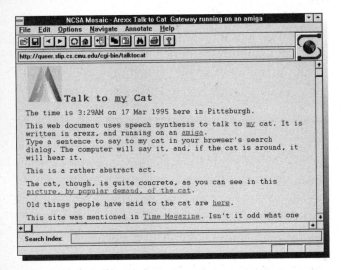

Here is yet another example of a human with too much control over his cat's Web page. When you tap into this page at Carnegie Mellon University in Pittsburgh you are invited to "talk to the cat." What happens is that when you type something into the page, a speech synthesizer on the computer on the other end blasts out your greeting, likely scaring some poor cat witless as he diligently types away at the computer's keyboard. Visit at

http://queer.slip.cs.cmu.edu/cgi_bin/talktocat

Steve

In the status-conscious world of cat cyberspace, Steve the Cat is probably the most down-to-earth denizen. A randy fellow, he includes on his home page love letters he has received from Internet cat-babes, all annotated with his own wolfish comments. The page also includes a photojournalistic essay on how Steve likes to stand on top of doors. Press a button labeled What Steve Is Doing Now to see what activity the unpredictable Steve is engaged in at any given moment. Funny thing—he always appears to be sleeping. Visit Steve at

http://www.webcom.com/~feline/steve.html

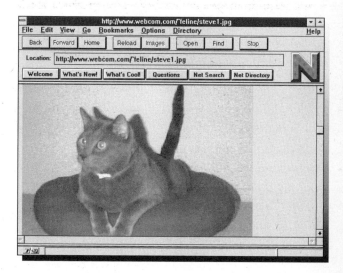

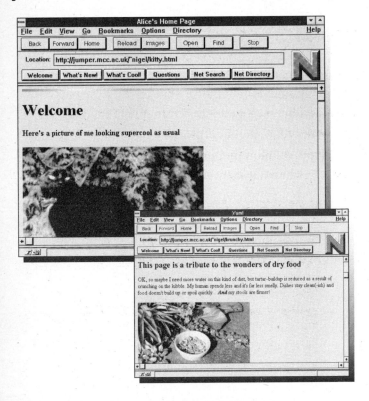

Nigel's page in Oxford, England, offers an intimate look at the life of a British cat. Nigel lists as his hobbies tripping humans, lying in "limpid pools of sunlight on soft duvets," and "being certain of my superiority to all and sundry." His page also includes a still-life photo, entitled "Tribute to Dry Cat Food," of a floral arrangement accessorized by his bowl of kibble. Visit Nigel at

http://jumper.mcc.ac.uk/~nigel/kitty.html

Tiger

Tiger's page features photos of its subject in two classic poses: patrolling the house and enjoying a contemplative moment at rest. Tiger begins the text portion of his page by coyly insisting that "being as shy as I am, I don't have much to say," but scroll down the page and you'll read his rich reminiscences of unrolling toilet paper. Visit Tiger at

**http://diablo.cpi.com/cpihtml/homepages/
edwards/tigerpic.html**

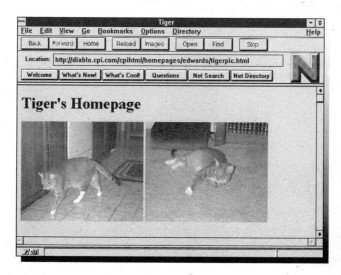

Ben and Izzy's home page is among the coziest on the Internet. They invite you to sign their guest book, either by typing your name or clicking on the "Paw Print" feature. Big photos of Ben and Izzy together with minimalist editorial content make viewing the page almost as gratifying as ogling cats in person. Visit Ben and Izzy at

http://www.rain.org/~jbrandon/cats.html

Don't let Max the dog scare you off. This Web site,
Pet Pages, is the most important one in the United
Kingdom. Here you'll meet dozens of gorgeous
cats from around the globe, including Angeline,
Boz, Bella, Zippy, and the inimitable Coo. Not only
can you see pictures of them, but they've included
their e-mail addresses so that you can write to them
too! This page is even better than a 900 fantasy-
friend chat number. If you'd like your picture
included on Pet Pages, e-mail a scanned photo of
yourself to **pets@manor.demon.co.uk.** Only GIF
or JPEG format graphics files 20K or smaller are
accepted.

**http://sashimi.wwa.com/~tenec/users/paulf/
pets/pets.html**

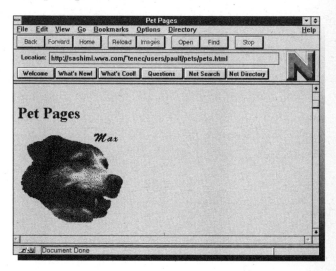

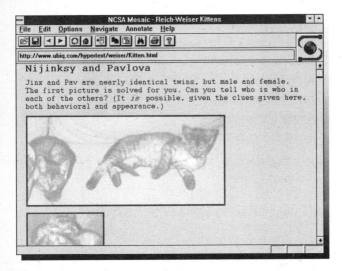

Nijinksy and Pavlova challenge you to tell them apart on their Web page. What a delightful activity to keep your mischief-prone human occupied for an evening! I'll give you a clue: Nijinksy is the cute one. Visit them at

**http://www.ubiq.com/hypertext/weiser/
kitten.html**

Orange

Orange has used sophisticated computer-art tech-
niques to create a Web page that is both thought-
provoking and visually exciting. Scroll down the
page for a picture of his food dish and a photojournalistic essay entitled "What I Like to Eat."
Orange's page also features the inevitable cheesecake photos of feline beauties. Visit Orange at

**http://www.halycon.com/manray/ian/orange/
orange.html**

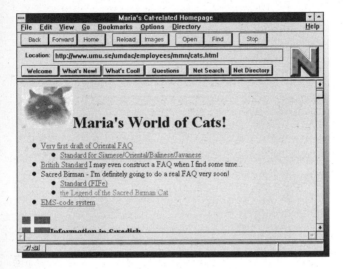

Tap into Maria's World of Cats and read the Legend of the Sacred Birman Cat while you ogle photos of Swedish cats like the delectable Spigg, also known as Bandar Shah's Signed Debutante. Yeow! Imagine running into this Nordic cat-babe late at night on an FTP server! You can read the page in English, but the Swedish version is more fun. Visit Maria at

http://www.umu/se/umdac/employees/mmn/ cats.html

Boris the Wonder Cat will amaze you with pictures of his daredevil feats. His page also includes pictures of his brainy sister Cutie Pie. Visit them at

http://bobcat.bbn.com/borispage.html

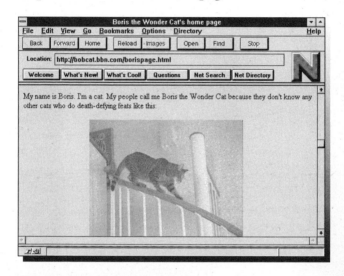

Monster's humans named him for his habit of waking them at 2:30 each morning to play. (Is it Monster's fault that his humans need more aerobic exercise?) His favorite hobby is ornithology, which he pursues daily from behind a window. Hear Monster's meow at

http://neon.cchem.berkeley.edu/~gezelter/ Monster.html

This exquisite beauty boasts a pedigreed look and a high-class name. Kaiun means *great fortune* in Japanese, something this cat has enjoyed since caring humans rescued her from a makeshift home outside a dumpster. Kaiun haunts the web at

http://www.pcnet.com/users/stenor/cats/ kaiun.html

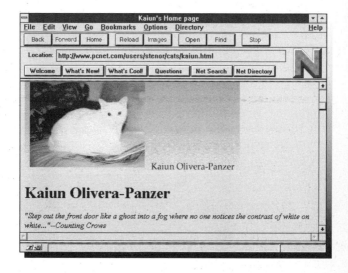

Chapter Four

Internet Catteries After Dark and Other Virtual Diversions for Cats

It's after midnight and you can't find a way out of the house to sing under the neighbor's bedroom window. The door's locked and your human's sleeping like the Rock of Gibraltar; not even stepping on his face would wake him. What to do? Log on to the Internet to prowl the electronic catteries, of course! This growing web of Internet-linked cat breeders serves up stunning digitized graphics of their pedigreed cat babes and tom toys. Who knows, you may just find the kitten of your dreams.

The I-way holds other late-night entertainments, too, like adventure games starring cats and virtual-reality fish tanks. So don't despair if you can't serenade the neighborhood at 2 a.m. with your own special rendition of "Ride of the Valkyries." Curl up on the keyboard, pull out the catnip mouse, and enjoy the wild life that the Internet offers wired cats like you.

Cattery

CAT-A-COMB

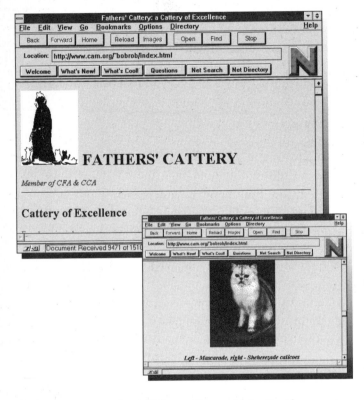

The monastic order of Notre Dame de la Confience in Quebec runs Fathers' Cattery. Their motto: "Our Aim Furrever—Purrfection in God's Loving Care." They specialize in breeding Persians and exotic shorthairs, which they train to obey commands and then give to senior citizens. (Who but a monk would try to train a cat?) Visit this divinely inspired cattery by pointing your Web walker to

http://www.cam.org/~bobrob/index.html

Cat Power User Tip
COMMANDEER A HOME OFFICE

More and more cats are finding a home office indispensable to their high-powered lifestyles. What is a home office? It's a quiet room that you appropriate for your own use. Ideally, it's equipped with a file cabinet to sleep on, business cards to scatter, an answering machine with lots of buttons to step on, and, of course, a computer. Never mind if your human chases you out of your office when you try to use it. You can always sneak back in at night when she's sleeping.

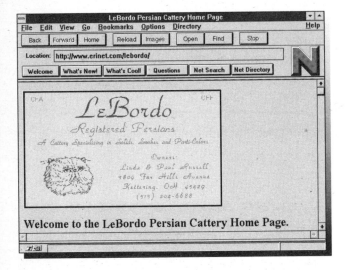

At LeBordo Cattery in Kettering, Ohio, all Persian cats are named after French Bordeaux wines. Click on their names to read their pedigrees.

http://www.erinet.com/lebordo/

Ylletrollet's Cattery

Fiery but sweet Kiss Me Kate is one of the stars of Ylletrollet's Cattery in Uppsala, Sweden. Her eyes sparkle with the romance of the Northern European Internet after dark. One of her mates is the Maine Coon Cat Stud of the Year Ec & Pr Caprix Blue Bogart "Bogi," father of 30 kittens. Unfortunately, his Web page says that he is now neutered. Visit Ylletrollet's Cattery at

http://www.tdb.uu.se/~peter/cats/ylletroll.html

Lady Godiva Cattery

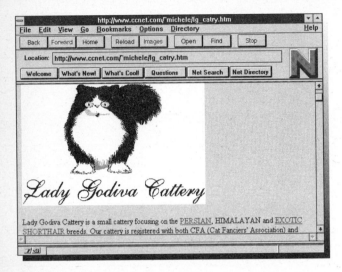

Pretty-pawed pussycats grace the rose bowers at the Lady Godiva Cattery. Join the party at

http://www.ccnet.com/~michele/lg_catry.html

Cat Net Surfer Tip

It's OK to mistake the cursor for a fly and leap up from the keyboard to whack at it.

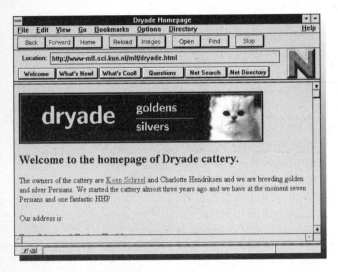

No need to cross the Atlantic to pay a call on fur-babies in the Netherlands. To initiate a digital tête-à-tête with the cybercats of this esteemed Dutch cattery point your Web walker to

http://www-mlf.sci.kun.nl/mlf/dryade.html

If you're ever lost in an avalanche in the Swiss Alps, forget the St. Bernards. Hope that your rescuer is one of these burly babes. Maine coon cats rule the cat trees at the Ambar Cattery in San Francisco. Visit them at

http://cesium.clock.org/~ambar/ambar.html

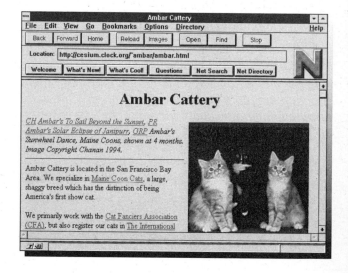

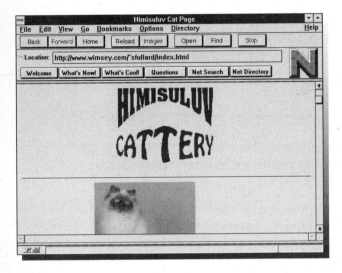

The Himisuluv Cattery in British Columbia specializes in breeding Himalayans. All that gorgeous fur should keep your keyboard toes warm in winter. *Prrrrrrrrrrr!* Introduce yourself to these pedigreed darlings (and learn more about Himalayans) at

http://www.wimsey.com/~sfullard/index.html

Everyone loves Bombay cats. Dapper, intelligent, and blessed with offbeat wit, they're the life of any party, either human or animal. Find Bombay party pals for your next bash at the Thomcats Cattery in Houston at

http://www.ai.mit.edu/fanciers/people/ thomcats.html

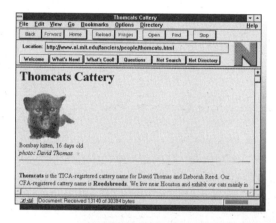

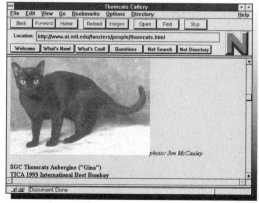

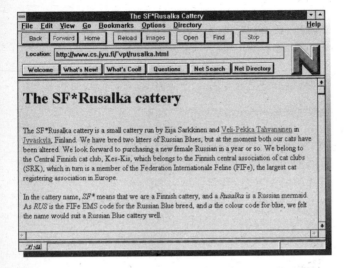

The SF*Rusalka Cattery in Finland specializes in raising Russian blue cats with magical eyes. Enter this fantastical cattery at

http://www.cs.jyu.fi/~vpt/rusalka.html

Maine coon cats are among the most popular breeds on the Internet. This may be because when one drops onto a keyboard the computer does surprising things (assuming the keyboard survives). Visit these zaftig felines at KamelotKoons at

http://www.csn.net/~petrdill/

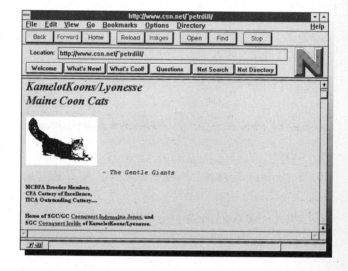

Lutece Incendiare and Lutece Ivoire of Ashmanor greet you at the Lutece Cattery home page in Boston. This esteemed cattery, bearing the medieval name of Paris, raises award-winning Chartreux cats like the venerable Lutece Hymne à la Joie, more familiarly known as Presto. Presto was the Cat Fanciers' Association National Best Chartreux of 1994. Needless to say, all the Lutece cats are multilingual and well versed in the fine arts. And they never fight; they hold civilized symposia instead. Be sure to brush up on your French before you visit them at

http://www.ai.mit.edu/fanciers/orca/lutece.html

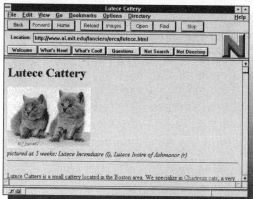

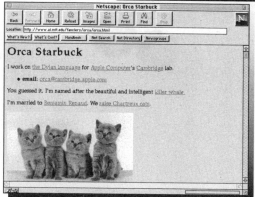

A Few More...

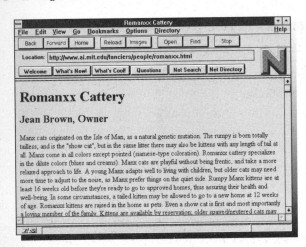

http://www.ai.mit.edu/fanciers/people/
romanxx.html

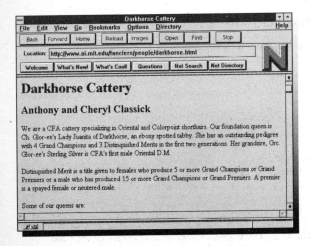

http://www.ai.mit.edu/fanciers/people/
darkhorse.html

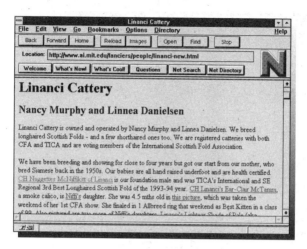

http://www.ai.mit.edu/fanciers/people/
linanci-new.html

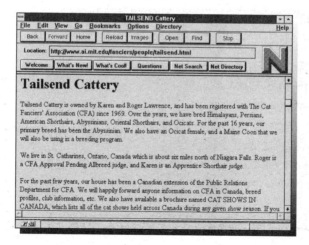

http://www.ai.mit.edu/fanciers/people/
tailsend.html

Cat Net Surfer Tip

You can find your way to more catteries on the Internet by heading to the Cat Fanciers' Home Page at

http://www.ai.mit.edu/fanciers/fanciers.html

The Amazing Fish Cam!

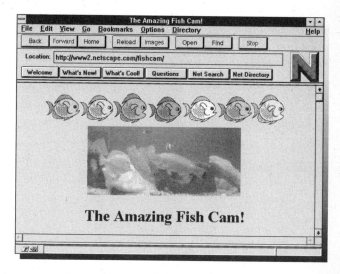

If your human won't set up a fish tank for you, head to the Fish Cam and gaze at the virtual fishies swimming over your computer screen. A camera connected to this Web page broadcasts digital images of a real fish tank every few minutes. Yum!

http://www2.netscape.com/fishcam/

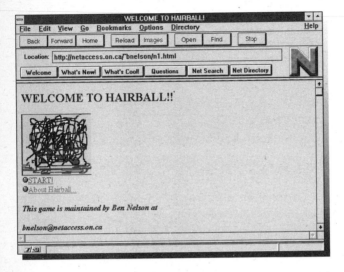

Hairball is an online adventure game for cats. The premise: You're on vacation with your humans, and they've left you at the hotel in the care of some boob security guard while they go swimming. (Not that you'd like to go swimming but, I mean, the nerve!) As the guard dozes, you escape from your cat carrier and head out on the town to track down your negligent family. Colorful pictures illustrate each turn in the adventure.

http://netaccess.on.ca/~bnelson/n1.html

Fuertes Bird Images

Brush up on your birding skills without getting a mouth full of feathers by heading to one of the many bird lovers' sites on the Internet. This one features paintings by artist Louis Agassiz Fuertes. Visit this site at

**http://oitnext.cit.cornell.edu/library-images/
fuertes-birds.html**

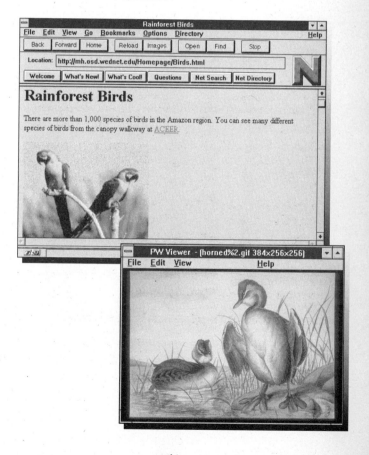

Chapter Five

CAT BOUTIQUES ON THE INFOBAHN

Shopping doesn't come naturally to most cats; we can't help thinking that anything we sit on is automatically ours. But shopping by computer can be rewarding, especially when you're using your human's credit card. It is normally highly ill advised to type your own credit-card number into an e-mail message or World Wide Web page, but who cares if a hacker steals your human's number?

You can buy all kinds of goodies on the Internet, from liver treats to herbal balms and cat-nip pillows. You can even buy gifts for your human, though you probably needn't bother since she can always drive herself to the mall. Cat boutiques pop up almost weekly on the World Wide Web. Many show pictures of their products and list 800 numbers for ordering.

Unfortunately, the Internet doesn't offer much in the way of cat fashions yet (I'm on the lookout for a little feather tiara for a certain Balinese minx I met on Mr. Puddy's Home Page), but hopefully more boutiques will spring up as merchants begin to realize the buying power of cats—especially those using computers.

Cat Faeries is a mail-order company operated by cybercat Betty Rushin' Blue. It specializes in products that "bring enchantments, good health, and happiness to cats and their humans." Among their specialties: "catnip dream pillows," "catnip flower essence," and cat-shaped mouse pads. Visit the Cat Faeries Web page at **http://slip-1.slip.net/ ~catfaeri/** or drop Betty an e-mail requesting a catalog (they're $1) at **catfaeri@slip.net.** You can also call her at 415-550-7472.

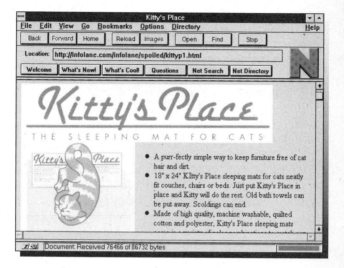

If you're tired of sleeping on that lumpy baby blanket, check out Kitty's Place Sleeping Mats at **http://infolane.com/infolane/spoiled/kittyp1. html**. These ergonomically designed mats will keep the creaks out of your back, and they're quilted for extra comfort. You can also call Kitty's Place at 415-321-5552 or write **fankmona@aol.com**.

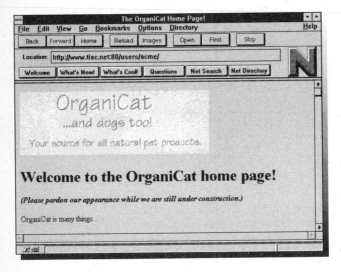

OrganiCat, run by a clowder of politically correct cats including Elvis and Gorbachev, specializes in natural pet products like organic canned food and herbal remedies. Visit OrganiCat at **http://www.tiac.net/users.acme** or e-mail **natracat@tiac.net.**

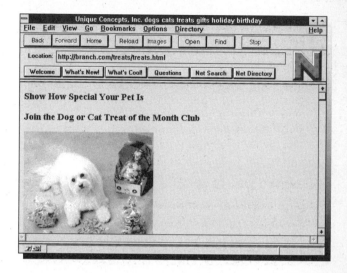

The Cat Treat of the Month Club will mail you a monthly surprise box of delectables for a mere $4.95 per month, plus $1.95 for shipping. You can tap into the club's Web page at **http://branch.com: 1080/treats/treats.html** or call 800-FUN-DOGS (an unfortunate choice in a vanity 800 number). Be sure you have your human's credit card handy when you call.

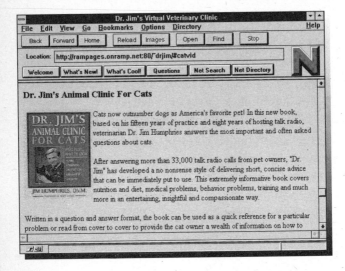

No matter what people say, we are not simple creatures. My human has long claimed that when I sleep on her head I sound like a diesel engine, but not until I logged onto this Web site did I learn that she wasn't just kvetching: We cats purr at 26 cycles per second, the same frequency as an idling engine. You'll read other fascinating tidbits at Dr. Jim's Virtual Veterinary Clinic at **http://rampages. onramp.net:80/~drjim/**. You can also order books and videos on cat behavior by talk-radio host and vet Jim Humphries. Give them as thoughtful gifts to the human in your life who still can't figure out why you refuse to use the cat box when it's filled with that green ecolitter. Dr. Jim's observations are keen—he understands that we cats don't like to do anything that's not our own idea. But be warned: Some of his ideas go too far. For instance, he tells humans that they can convince a cat to crawl into a cat carrier by making the cat think it was his idea. Horrifying!

Cat Net Surfer Tip

Have notices about cat products deposited directly in your private e-mail box by joining the Pet Info Mailing List. Send an e-mail message to listserv@netcom.com. Type anything you like as the subject; the message itself should contain only the line **subscribe pet-info-l**

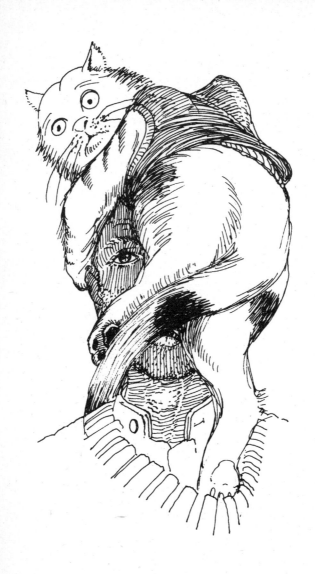

Part Two

Internet Help for Humans

(heaven knows, they need it)

Chapter Six

INTERNET
HAUNTS FOR CATS
AND HUMANS

The Internet hosts many places where cats and humans commune. The most horrifying (to us cats, at least) of these is Usenet, a big collection of public discussion groups or *newsgroups*. But Usenet has one big problem: It's full of humans. If it were full of animals it would be more interesting. Not only that, but it contains only one newsgroup for cats (it has seven for dogs). And to top it off, the cat newsgroup is cluttered with kibble-brained people who flood the Internet with bonehead theories about why their cats lick walls, as if there were anything wrong with that.

So if you're looking for some fun Usenet newsgroups, all you'll find is rec.pets.cats. I say avoid rec.pets.cats. Instead, head to rec.pets.dogs. There you can type withering messages like "I know a dog who is so stupid that he barks when his tail hits the walls because he thinks it's a burglar."

Note: If after these admonitions you still want to check out rec.pets.cats, and you subscribe to an online service like CompuServe or America Online, you can get there by using the service's Go, Jump, or Keyword feature. Type either **usenet** or **internet**, then select Usenet from the menu that appears. Search the newsgroups for rec.pets.cats, then click on Subscribe to read the messages posted there. Avoid messages entitled "How to Bathe a Cat."

On the Internet, No One Knows You're a Dog, But If You're a Cat...

There is a popular saying on the Internet: No one knows you're a dog, but everyone knows what your cat looks like. Not surprisingly, lots of messages describing cats flit back and forth over the Internet. To prevent phrases like *long tail* and *whiskers full of lint* from clogging the information highway, cat worshippers have created a lexicon of special abbreviations to describe the cats that keep them. They're called Usenet cat codes, and they sign their e-mail with them. For instance, my human would sign her e-mail this way:

> Sincerely,
>
> Judy
>
> Bubbles: DS (R+W)t G 15 Y+ L+++ W++ C+++ I++ T A–––
> E++ H S+ V++ F+ Q++ P++ B PA PL

These codes tell you that I am an orange-and-white mackerel tabby with the size and disposition of a mountain lion (though I occasionally like my belly rubbed). The codes also describe my tastes in females, my hunting propensities, and under what circumstances I will fetch a ball.

For instance, DS stands for domestic shorthair, (R+W)t means red-and-white tabby, G means green eyes, 15 is my age, and so forth. Codes describing personality come toward the end. PA and PL refer to purr quality and volume level, P++ means that I'm a lap fungus (a bit of Internet human slang for a cat that suffers emotional distress when removed from a warm lap). Q++ means I'm capable of abstract reasoning (in other words, I know where to go when it's time for a nap). A– – – is my human's assessment of my activity level— she's saying that I could be mistaken for dead unless I hear the can opener.

Make sure your human learns these codes so they can sign their e-mail appropriately. The full list can be found in the Appendix.

I have developed my own set of codes to describe humans. But since their personalities are so simple compared with cats', the codes are shorter. I hope that one day my human codes acquire as much popularity on the Internet as the cat codes. I like to sign my e-mail messages this way:

Catch ya' in the bitstream, baby!

Bubbles

Judy: (eau de Head and Shoulders)No-sardines[zip-sanity] <hu-choo!>

From the above you can tell that my Internet slave's scalp smells peculiar, she's too cheap to buy sardines, she calls me an obstruction to sanity when she pulls me off the keyboard, and she once sprayed my carpet-covered cat tree with Lysol.

The full list of Internet cat codes is regularly posted in the Usenet newsgroup rec.pets.cats. The list is maintained by a human, Eric Williams, who labors in the employ of a cybercat named Sapphyr. In fact, Sapphyr did the HTML coding for the World Wide Web page that also lists the codes (**http://turnpike.net/metro/sapphyr/catcode. html**). You can also download the code list via anonymous FTP at ftp.netcom.com. Head to the directory **pub/wd/wd6cmu/cats/catcode** for the file. Warning: This list is the size of a computer-repair manual, not surprising considering how complex we cats are.

Advanced Keyboard Trick
HELP YOUR HUMAN EXIT HER APPLICATION WITHOUT SAVING HER WORK

Sometimes you'll find your Internet slave wasting time creating spreadsheets when she should be paying attention to you. Correct this oversight by taking a flying leap at the computer from the nearest high object and knocking the keyboard to the floor. As you and the keyboard fly through the air, rotate your body so that both of you back-flip just before hitting the carpet. Once you've mastered this maneuver, try yowling and pulling the mouse down with you. Get all tangled up in the cords and start running crazily around the room. You'll so alarm your human that she'll forget about the spreadsheet she just lost and immediately pick you up to console you.

125

INTERNET MAILING LISTS FOR CATS

In addition to the rec.pets.cats newsgroup, the Internet boasts a number of other cat-related discussion groups that both you and your human might enjoy. These are quasi-private conversations called mailing lists. You can subscribe to them from any commercial online or Internet service by sending an Internet message to the person or computer running the list. Once you're signed up, you'll receive the rules for the list as well as all its messages in your private e-mailbox. Depending upon the list, the number of people and cats participating in the discussion may be huge, and you may receive from two messages a day to hundreds. (By the way, be sure your human reads the list's rules and prints them for future reference. Of course you won't need the rules because, as a cat, you don't have to follow them.)

Meet Cool Cybercats and Their Internet Slaves in Feline-L

One of the most powerful political entities on the Internet are the cat lovers who commune daily via the mailing list Feline-L. Each week they share important information, like how to fix gourmet meals for their cats (they each have at least five), how to kiss cats, and how to get cat smells out of couch pillows. Cats join in the conversation too, tapping in messages about fish and fur beds and organizing virtual reality pizza parties. (You'll know that a cat has joined the conversation when you spot messages with CATCHAT in the subject.)

To sign up, send an e-mail message to **listserv@psuvm.psu.edu** with whatever you want in the subject line. The only thing you should type in the body of the message is the line **subscribe feline-l** *Firstname Lastname*—for example, **subscribe feline-l Bubbles Rodilardus**. You'll receive a confirmation message in reply. Respond with another message consisting of only the word **OK.** You can send a message to all the cats and humans on this mailing list by addressing it to **feline-l@psuvm.psu.edu.**

Watch People Entertain Themselves with Cute Cat Stories in Cats-L

People never seem to run out of charming stories about us. This is especially true of the Internet slaves who commune via the mailing list Cats-L. Each day they naively ponder why their cats stare at them icily whenever they sleep in (because breakfast is late, you fool!) or why their cats sometimes appear to disdain them (because you left the Cat-Dancer toy in the garden when we wanted to play in the living room, pizza-brain!). Many of this list's members are librarians who log in from work, so forgive them their lapses as servants—they have enough trouble keeping riff-raff like voles and grackles out of the card catalog when we're not around to help.

To join our adoring fans on Cats-L, send an e-mail message to **listserv@netcom.com,** with whatever you want in the subject line. The only thing you should type in the body of the message is the line **subscribe cats-l**. Once you're signed up, you can send messages to everyone on the list by addressing your message to **cats-l@netcom.com.**

Cat Net Surfer Tip

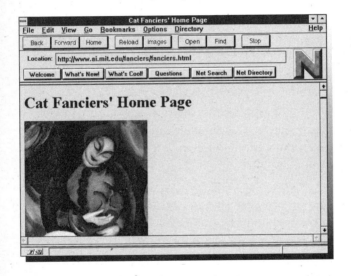

The Cat Fanciers' Mailing List maintains a World Wide Web site that you can use as a springboard for reaching just about anything on the Internet related to cats, from veterinary advice and breed information to glamour shots of exquisite cats. Tap in by pointing your Web walker to

http://www.ai.mit.edu/fanciers/fanciers.html

Pick Up Cat Beauty Secrets in the Cat Fanciers' List

If you think you can stroll into a cat show and win a wheelbarrow full of ribbons just by licking yourself clean, think again. Raking in the booty on the cat-show circuit requires perspiration and preparation on your human's part. For starters, you'll need cat-tray liners that match the tieback curtains on your cage. Then there are bubble baths, preferably a different one for each color in your coat (a soap with a color-enhancing agent for your black spots, one with blueing agents for your white spots, and so on). And don't forget to attach a sign to your cage warning showgoers, "Do not poke fingers in cage. The magnificent creature inside may claw your arm off."

If you aspire to hit the show circuit, make the Cat Fanciers' List your first stop. You'll learn more about cat shows here than you will just about anywhere else in the world. You'll also be privy to the dramas surrounding the lives of other show cats, like the peculiar eye goobers that plague a cat named Madonna Louise after breeding.

The Cat Fanciers' List is a private mailing list; to join you must send a personal note to Orca Starbuck (**fanciers-request@ai.mit.edu**), who runs the list. Tell her how serious you are about cat shows and how you and your human fit into the scene—whether you're a show cat, an aspiring stud, or a litter-box hanger-on. If you're accepted, make sure your human reads the list rules (no cute cat stories allowed), and be warned that message traffic on this list is heavy—a recent message entitled "Tummy Troubles" generated about 5,000 messages. Once you've subscribed, you can send a message to everyone on the list by addressing it to **fanciers@ai.mit.edu.**

This list is run by a computer in the Massachusetts Institute of Technology's artificial intelligence lab, clearly one research institute that understands the importance of beautiful cats to the future of American technology.

Learn How to Run a Cat Bed-and-Breakfast in Cattery-L

If you plan to turn your human's house into a shelter for homeless neighborhood cats or if you just plan to invite a lot of friends in, sign up your human for the Cattery-L mailing list, a discussion group devoted to "cat management" (perish the thought). Cattery-L is for anyone who breeds cats, runs hotel accommodations for cats, or otherwise harbors so many cats that he thinks he's going insane.

You'll meet many overworked cat servants on Cattery-L, but don't feel sorry for them. In addition to having a dozen or more cats to entertain them, most have their own mattresses that they can sleep on in a corner of the house amid the foam cat beds. And all appear reasonably competent at using a litter scoop. They are a resourceful bunch, and your Internet slave will appreciate being put in contact with others who also have a hard time keeping the house from smelling like a giant litter box.

To join, send an Internet e-mail message to **listserv@netcom.com.** Put whatever you want in the subject line. Type **subscribe cattery-l** in the body of the message. To send a message to everyone on the mailing list, address it to **cattery-l@netcom.com.**

Cybernetwork with the King of Beasts in Felines-L

Ever wonder how the big cats live? If so, sign up for the Felines-L mailing list (not to be confused with Feline-L, described above). Run by Cornell University, this list is devoted to discussing lifestyle and preservation issues for lions, panthers, tigers, mountain lions, and other big cats (which we all could be if only we could find time in our rigorous nap schedules to use the Soloflex). Traffic is light on this list, so don't worry if you don't see any messages for several weeks.

To join, send an Internet e-mail message to **listserv@cornell.edu.** Put whatever you want in

the subject line and type **subscribe felines-l**
Firstname Lastname in the body of the message.
Once you're signed up, you'll receive a list of the
Latin taxonomic names of 37 species in the *Felidae*
family, along with specifics on body and tail sizes
and habitat. Print this out so that your human can
memorize it. To send a message to everyone on the
list, address it to **felines-l@cornell.edu.**

Learn About Natural Pet Care

Worried that your litter-box clay may be causing
those hemorrhoids? Curious about "flower remedies" and whether they can cure what ails you?
Sign up for the Natural Pet Care list to learn about
organic cat food, holistic vets, acupuncture, and
other natural alternatives to conventional pet-care
products. This is a fairly active list, so expect a lot
of mail.

To join, send an Internet e-mail address to
listserv@netcom.com. Put whatever you want in
the subject line but be sure to type **subscribe
natrlpet-l** in the body of the message. Send a message to everyone on the mailing list by addressing it
to **natrlpet-l@netcom.com.**

*By the way, once you're signed up for all these mail-
ing lists, you'll get thousands of messages, which will
overflow your mailbox. Don't worry. And don't concern
yourself with the fact that these messages may fill up the
computer's hard disk, causing "Warning! Disk full!"
errors when your human tries to save his spreadsheet.*

Rest assured that your human will find time to clean up the mess as he goes about his daily ritual of straightening picture frames, wiping cat-food crumbs off the floor, and duct-taping the rips in the couch arms.

INTERNET CAT SLANG

Humans use many terms of endearment when writing e-mail about us. Here are some of them, along with other bits of slang found in areas of the Internet where cats and their humans congregate.

D*g   Variant spelling of the name of that dull-witted, drooling species with four feet and a tail whose idea of an intellectual challenge is rolling in the dirt without hurting himself. The asterisk is used to avoid typing obscenities in public e-mail.

Lap fungus   A cat who suffers severe physical maladies when removed from the warm lap where he is sleeping. Symptoms may include stiff back, ataxia, and creaky tail. The only remedy is to return the cat immediately to the lap and to stroke his back gently. Allow the cat to remain on the lap for several hours, or until he removes himself.

Smurgle   What cats do to humans to prevent them from pining away with loneliness and despair over how empty their lives would be without us. Usually involves purring, kneading, and snuggling on the part of the cat, chin scratching and fur stroking on the part of the human.

Fur-baby   Sentimental term used by humans to refer to the only creature that will ever give their lives meaning. A variant of the term coined by the late May Sarton in her famous novel about a gentleman cat, *The Fur Person.*

Rainbow Bridge   Where cats are said to go when we die. The term comes from a popular tale called "Rainbow Bridge," widely circulated on the Internet (you'll find a version of it in the Appendix). It's nice to think that we go to the end of the rainbow, but everyone knows that when cats die we don't go to some creaky bridge to hang out with a bunch of dead dogs. We enjoy luxury accommodations that make Versailles look like a Motel 6, where we spend the day snoozing on Queen Anne divans, climbing opulent drapes, and clawing the heck out of golden tapestries woven by angels just for us. Rainbow Bridges with mutts, indeed! *Harrrummmph!*

Internet Cat Graffiti

We cats are perfect works of art. Our images adorn temples, pyramids, picture books, and T-shirts. Our pictures grace the lines of e-mail too. Granted, the ASCII-character art stamped at the bottom of electronic messages is somewhat unsophisticated compared with the paintings of Renoir and Gauguin. But as tributes to our impish spirit, they transcend their crudeness. Here are some of the more inspired pictograms I have sent and received, along with favorite Internet sayings pertaining to cats.

```
   |  \  _  /  |
   |  o     o  |
  ==\  _x_  /==
```

All intelligent species in the universe
are owned by cats.

```
  |         /\_/\
  |         (- -)
  \_——-=\"/=
   |  _____  /
   | |         | |
   | |         | |
   ^ ^         ^ ^
```

Whatever you're doing, it's not as
important as petting the cat.

```
 |\___/|
>> 0 0 <<
  =={+}===      #
   /`  ^  '\      ##
  /     v    \   ##
 |   | | |   |  ##
 |   | | |   | ##
 |__mm mm__|#
```

Purr, and the world purrs with you.
Hiss, and you hiss alone.

```
  A.,.A
 (u u )\-=-__--===-.
  `.^,,'   ,      (      \`-.
/~/~~~~~ /...;/~~~~~   (`\`.
```

Those who dislike cats will be carried to the
cemetery in the rain.—Dutch proverb

```
  /\_/\
 ( 0.0 )
  > 0 <
```

The cat made me write this!

```
        /\___/\                    /\___/\
      ( o     o )               ( o       o )
      (    =^=    )             (    =^=      )
      (            )            (              )
    (    | |      )            (    | |        )
      (   ( (                   (   ( (       ))))
                                 ))))))))))))
```

The opinions expressed above are not those of
my employer, family, friends, relations, or myself.
They come from my cats.—Standard Internet-
style message disclaimer

```
        /\___/\
       |  . .  |
      (__>^<__)
        (        )   /~
        (          )/
      (_)_____(_)
```

What's virtue in man can't be vice in a cat.
—Mary Abigail Dodge

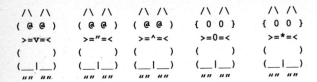

> "I love my cats because I love my home"
> —Jean Cocteau

Only a life lived for cats is a life worth living.

Roller-Kitty!!!

God created cats so that man might enjoy
the pleasure of caressing the tiger.

```
    _/\_/\_          _/\_/\_
    \ o o /          \ o o /
     >>*<<            >>o<<

 _/\_/\_          _/\_/\_          _/\_/\_
 \ o o /          \ o o /          \ - - /
  >>o<<            >>-<<            >>o<<
```

If you want to be loved, be lovable.—Ovid

Purrrr...

Cat Power User Tip

Do Not Mistake the Mouth of a Laser Printer for a Mouse Hole

During their first session at the computer, many cats mistake the paper slot in the printer for the door to a mouse hole. Some cats who fall victim to this delusion waste futile hours waiting in vain for the paper to re-emerge.

Don't let this happen to you. Remember: when something disappears into a computer, it usually does not reappear. Not unless it is pried out with a violence that would make you lose claws and fur in the process. Or unless the computer spits it out, in which case you probably won't want it anyway.

Cat Power User Tip

MAKE SURE YOU HAVE A NAP SPOT CLOSE TO THE COMPUTER

While the tops of printers and monitors are warm places to nap, be sure that you have additional nap spots near the computer. As we know, intense mental exertion can quickly send us into a near-comatose state. While the computer chair is always convenient for napping (especially if someone is about to sit in it), you should have other nap spots, too. Look for spots far from drafts, like the insides of computer boxes. If your human is a true computer geek, you may even find a basket of unsorted laundry near the computer, which makes an especially cozy sleeping spot.

Cat Net Surfer Tip

There is a secret place on the Internet where homeless cats find new homes. Caring humans communicate via private e-mail to relay cats cross-country to new digs using a system they call the cat underground railroad. Frankly, I think it would be wiser to relocate the humans instead, but I suspect shipping costs would be prohibitive.

chapter seven

FINDING SMART
VETS AND
PRACTICAL
MEDICAL ADVICE
IN CYBERSPACE

I t's 3 a.m. and you think you're suffering from radiation sickness. After all, you fell off the computer monitor twice while taking a nap that day—and isn't it true that these monitors leak electromagnetic frequency rays?

Or maybe your tail is acting funny. It keeps hopping around. You smack it down with a paw, but it keeps twitching. You wonder if you're developing a rare disease—perhaps it's scurvy (your human did just change your food to something that tastes like freezer-burned bologna).

What to do? If you're like a growing number of cats, you log onto the Internet and scan its many databases for information on your symptoms.

Note: Despite popular misconceptions, cats are not hypochondriacs. Rather, we're sensitive creatures who like to be informed consumers of the veterinarian health-care system.

The Internet and commercial online services are excellent sources of cat health-care information, whether you're seeking special diets for feline urinary-tract disorder or want to know how much rest you need after that hooligan tabby down the street has bitten your tail. You can consult with vets online and scan databases at almost every major veterinary school in the United States (and many abroad as well) for reference material. You can even chat with other cats afflicted with the same maladies as you.

Best of all, you can access almost all of this medical information by heading to just one place on the Internet: a service called NetVet.

NetVet: One-Stop Shopping for Cat Health Care Info

NetVet is almost a small-scale online service in and of itself. Run by veterinarian Ken Boschert from Washington University in St. Louis, this remarkable resource gives cats, humans, and vets access to every piece of information related to animals and veterinary practice that can be found on the Internet. It also features some of the most gorgeous computer graphics on the Net (barring the various cat home pages, of course).

You reach information you want by clicking on icons. NetVet whisks you around the world to the information you seek, whether it's at a veterinary school in Michigan or a specialized medical journal.

You can tap into more than 20 vet schools through NetVet, although the average cat won't find much of interest in their collections, most of which consist of faculty rosters and campus descriptions instead of research reports and health databases. I suspect these write-ups have been posted to dissuade cats from taking up residence on the campuses, since most conspicuously fail to mention amenities like the size of the squirrel population and the number of overstuffed chairs in the faculty lounge. Some of these schools are so canary-brained that they offer links to computers at Harvard Medical School, which everyone knows suffers credibility problems since it lacks a teaching hospital dedicated to cats.

Big Databases for Little Paws

Fortunately, NetVet offers more than links to vet schools. Its Virtual Library showcases journals and textbooks, the text of animal-related laws, and superb info-files on specific topics like feline leukemia. The content ranges from digitized medical images (there's a Dog Abdomen series—not for the squeamish) to fun things like David Letterman's "Top 10 Signs That You've Gone to a Bad Veterinarian." (Unfortunately, the list omits vets who don't check to see if you've been abducted by aliens since the last visit.) NetVet also lets you run gopher searches of the Internet for more information and download veterinarian-related files using FTP.

Cat Net Surfer Tip

Gopher is a way of "burrowing" from one computer to another through the Internet to find information. It's easy to use, and you don't have to chase any gophers through drain pipes. Gopher lets you access much of the information available to you on the World Wide Web, but you can't view the lovely screens because gopher doesn't support the Internet's graphics. To use gopher, head to your service's main Internet menu then select the gopher menu and type in the gopher address of your destination. Once you're connected, menus guide you through the service, from reference works to veterinary schools around the world. If you start your gophering by heading to NetVet, you can "gopher" your way to other veterinary schools by merely picking choices off menus.

This is what a gopher menu looks like. Disappointing, isn't it? You'd think that with a name like gopher it would at least flit across the lawn and disappear down a hole.

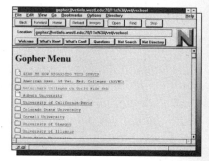

You can access NetVet several ways: by tapping directly into the Internet or using the Internet link of any major commercial online service; through the World Wide Web (point your Web crawler to **http://netvet.wustl.edu/**); or, if you don't have World Wide Web access, through gopher. NetVet's gopher address is **vetinfo.wustle.edu**. Access to NetVet is free except for any tolls you may incur from your online service.

It's 9:55 a.m. and in five minutes the vet is coming to pick you up to be neutered. You have never heard of this practice called neutering. To find out more, log into NetVet's World Wide Web site at **http://netvet.wustl.edu**, where you can access any veterinary information available on the Internet throughout the world. You may be surprised.

No, you're not neurotic if you log into NetVet eight or nine times a day to check your latest symptoms.

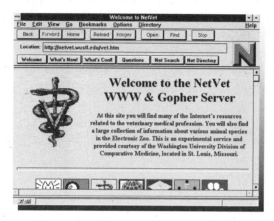

Click on NetVet's Electronic Zoo icon to search for information pertaining to cats. You'll find veterinary information as well as fun stuff, like cat humor and directions to Web pages decorated with Kliban cats.

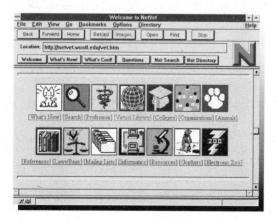

It is sad when cats are grouped on the same menu as cows and ferrets. Click the cat icon to escape the rabble and go straight to the cat stuff.

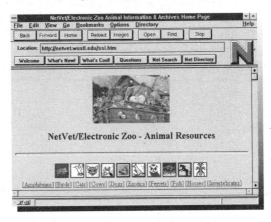

I've written Dr. Boschert a dozen times but he still won't give me the e-mail address of this cutie-pie gracing the welcome screen of NetVet's cat library. Maybe you'll have better luck.

Head to the Electronic Zoo on NetVet for a list of all the service's resources.

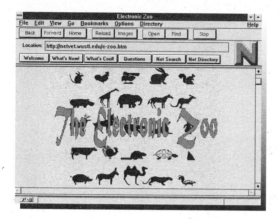

Cat Power User Tip
Do Not Fall Off
the Computer

M ost Quasi-Comatose Cybercat Topples
(QCCTs) occur when the victim falls asleep
while sitting on the monitor. But QCCT is easy to
prevent. Before you doze off on the computer,
make sure your entire body is on solid plastic and
that no part of it hangs over
the edge. For added
safety, fold your front
paws over the edge
of the monitor,
rest your head
on your paws,
and stretch your
behind out over
the air vents.
That way, if the
monitor over-
heats and catches
fire, you'll feel it
in time to escape.

FREE ADVICE FROM THE INTERNET VET

One of the best things about the Internet is that you can get veterinary advice without being stuffed into a cat carrier. In the quasi-monthly Internet Vet Column, Dr. Jeff Parke of Seattle answers such compelling questions as, "Will I grow an extra toe if I eat big black bugs off the sidewalk?" You can read his columns in several ways: on NetVet; as messages posted regularly in the Usenet discussion group rec.pets.cats; at his World Wide Web site (**http://www.io.com/user/tittle/ivc/homepage.html**), which contains past and current columns; or in your e-mailbox each week if you subscribe to the Internet Vet Column mailing list. To sign up, send an e-mail to **listserv@netcom.com.** Put whatever you want in the subject line and type **subscribe internet-vet-column *yourmailaddress*** in the body of the message, as in subscribe **internet-vet-column Bubbles@chessycat.edu.** To submit a question to the column, send it to **internet-vet@netcom.com.**

Internet Vet is not a discussion mailing list, so the only mail you will receive is the column. Also, because so many questions are asked, the Internet Vet cannot answer e-mail personally, no matter how many symptoms of rare cat diseases you claim to suffer from.

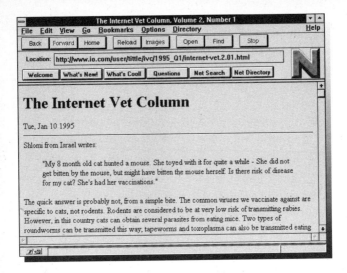

The Internet Vet Column, Volume 2, Number 1

File   Edit   View   Go   Bookmarks   Options   Directory   Help

Back   Forward   Home   Reload   Images   Open   Find   Stop

Location: http://www.io.com/user/tittle/ivc/1995_Q1/internet-vet.2.01.html

Welcome   What's New!   What's Cool!   Questions   Net Search   Net Directory

The Internet Vet Column

Tue, Jan 10 1995

Shlomi from Israel writes:

"My 8 month old cat hunted a mouse. She toyed with it for quite a while - She did not get bitten by the mouse, but might have bitten the mouse herself. Is there risk of disease for my cat? She's had her vaccinations."

The quick answer is probably not, from a simple bite. The common viruses we vaccinate against are specific to cats, not rodents. Rodents are considered to be at very low risk of transmitting rabies. However, in this country cats can obtain several parasites from eating mice. Two types of roundworms can be transmitted this way; tapeworms and toxoplasma can also be transmitted eating

You can read past installments of the Internet Vet Column by pointing your Web walker to **http://www.io.com/user/tittle/ivc/.** Most of the questions Dr. Parke addresses pertain to cats, but be warned: He occasionally descends into incoherent insanity and talks about dogs.

Cat Net Surfer Tip

If you're sitting on the keyboard and the computer starts beeping relentlessly, don't move. Curl your tail and look around innocently. It's not your fault.

THERE ARE OTHER PLACES ON THE INFO HIGHWAY WHERE VETS WILL ANSWER YOUR QUESTIONS, NO MATTER HOW DUMB

Cats in need of medical advice have even more Internet options than NetVet and the Internet Vet. Vets regularly log on to both America Online and CompuServe to answer subscribers' questions on everything from medical to behavioral problems. While you need an account on one of these services to access these resources (you can't just stroll in through the Internet), consulting with their online vets doesn't cost anything beyond the services' hourly connect fees.

To find the vets on CompuServe, log on and type the Go word **petsone**. Look for the category Ask-A-Vet in the messages. On America Online, type the keyword **pets**, then click on Petcare Message Center once you arrive in the forum. Under Categories, choose Questions for Vets. Check back regularly once you've sent your message since your question may not be answered for a week or more. I like the Ask-A-Vet service on America Online the best, and I also value all the cat medical advice shared by other subscribers. It's well worth the monthly fee.

Cat-Med

Symptom/Ailment DataBase

If your human won't give you Internet access, fire up this little $15 shareware database for PCs called Cat-Med instead. Tell it your symptoms, and it lists possible ailments. Cat-Med will also tell you if you're likely to be contagious to humans or other cats. You can download it from most computer services or get it through the Internet via NetVet. Look for the file CATMED20.ZIP. You can also order it from Jim Lynch: Write to P.O. Box 140192, Staten Island, NY 10314; e-mail **71210.2354@compuserve.com**; or phone 800-242-4775 (have a credit card ready).

Chapter Eight

Internet Cat FAQ Goddesses Offer Advice on Love, Life, Cat Toys, and How to Live with a Human Without Going Insane

We cats may be more misunderstood than any other creatures. I remember the time I spent hours redecorating the den only to hear my human shriek, "Migod, you clawed the wallpaper off the wall!" Then there was the time my humans absurdly insisted that toilet paper should stay on the roll, despite my attempt to enlighten them by unrolling it all on the floor.

For cyber-cats who must endure dysfunctional families, the Internet offers a treasure trove of lifestyle advice. It can be found in computer files called FAQs, for *frequently asked questions.* These are compilations of questions and answers that cats (and humans) regularly ask on the Internet. In the cat-oriented FAQ files, topics span from what a human should know before becoming emotionally involved with a cat to traveling with humans without going insane.

The authors are volunteers who spend hours collecting advice; I call them Cat FAQ Goddesses. They dispense tips on everything from how your humans can convince the landlord to let *you* live in the apartment even though *they're* the ones who are likely to make the mess, to choosing a vet (look for one who calls you Your Highness while she removes you gently from the cat carrier, not one who turns the carrier upside-down to shake you out). You'll find FAQs devoted to specific breeds, flea and tick eradication, and general cat care.

Note: Sadly, some cat FAQs propagate grievous untruths. For example, one labels cats' tendencies to climb drapes, chew electrical cords, and disrupt bird feeders as "behavior problems." Another advises humans who are allergic to their cat to spritz kitty with distilled water, when all they need do is wear a deep sea-diving mask with a clothespin on their nose.

These FAQs may prove your most valuable information source on the Internet next to conversations with other cats. There are more than 20 cat FAQs and several ways to get them: through the World Wide Web, FTP, and e-mail. Some are also posted as messages each month in the Usenet discussion group news.answers. Not all can be found on the same Internet sites, for they spring from different authors and sources.

You Can Get Cat FAQs Through the World Wide Web

The easiest way to get FAQs is through the World Wide Web. You can find most of them on the home page of Internet FAQ cat goddess Cindy Tittle Moore (she has written most of them, some with coauthor Erin Rebecca Miller at the University of Chicago). To get to Cindy's page, point your Web browser to **http://www.io.com/user/tittle/cats-faq/homepage.html**.

Another repository of FAQs, especially breed-specific ones, is the home page of the Cat Fanciers' Mailing List. Orca Starbuck, another FAQ cat goddess, runs this page from MIT. To get there, point your Web walker to **http://www.ai.mit.edu/fanciers/fanciers.html**. You'll find FAQs on Japanese bobtail and tricolor-coated cats (that's the one on cat genetics), plus one on Tonkinese cats. FAQ cat goddess Erin Miller's home page (**http://www.tezcat.com/~ermiller/FIP.shtml**) offers one on feline infectious peritonitis.

For a FAQ on Turkish angora cats, hop to **http://cesium.clock.org/~ambar/ta-faq.html**. At present this FAQ isn't available anywhere else.

You can find most of the FAQs devoted to individual cat breeds at Cindy Tittle Moore's page at **http://io.com/user/tittle/cats-faq-breeds/homepage.html**.

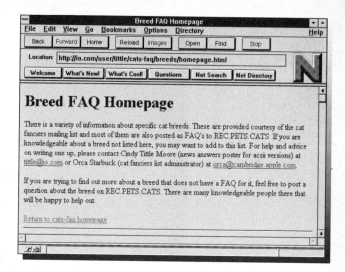

Log on to the Himalayan Cats Info Page at
http://www.wimsey.com/~sfullard/himi.html for
information about this sublime breed.

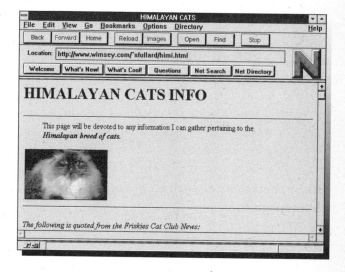

Cat Net Surfer Tip

Don't stare at the star-field screen saver so long that you feel like you're going to puke.

Sharing one's home with a cat comes with many responsibilities. This FAQ (**http://io.com/user/tittle/cats-faq/getting-a-cat.html**) spells out some of them for humans, though it fails to mention some of the more critical ones, like ridding the house of children, spouses, or other irritating creatures. And, when it calculates the expense of living with a cat, it doesn't include the cost of sheepskin fur throws for the cat carrier or the weekly fresh salmon.

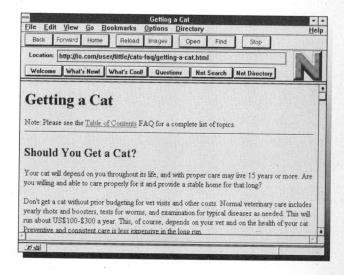

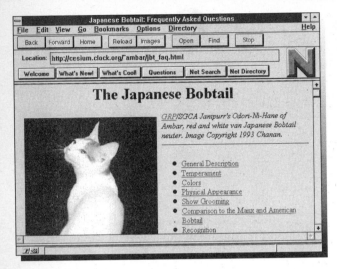

Get a copy of the Japanese bobtail FAQ from the World Wide Web page at **http://cesium.clock.org/~ambar/jbt_faq.html**. Click on any of the items listed on the page for more information.

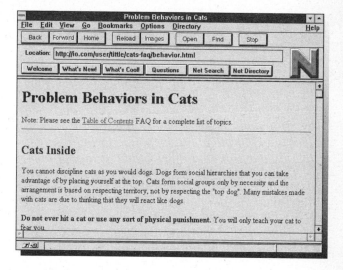

One of the most prevalent myths on Internet is that cats suffer from behavioral problems. This FAQ lists "cures" for supposed bad habits like climbing drapes, jumping on counters, and ripping new couches to shreds. You can download it from **http://io.com/user/tittle/cats-faq/behavior.html** or get a copy of it by e-mail. To receive it by e-mail, send an e-mail message to **mail-server@rtfm.mit.edu.** Your request will be processed by a computer so the only line in the message should be **send usenet/news.answers/cats-faq/behavior**

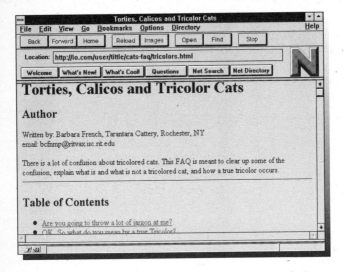

Humans claim that cats with the red gene (like myself) tend to throw temper tantrums and are unpredictable. Get the facts by reading the Torties, Calicos and Tricolor Cats FAQ (also known as the genetics FAQ). You can download it from **http://io.com/user/tittle/cats-faq/tricolor.html** or get a copy of it by e-mail. To receive it by e-mail, send a personal note requesting it to its author, Barbara French, at **bcfnmp@ritvax.isc.rit.edu.**

Cat Net Surfer Tip

Head to my home page at http://execpc.com/ ~judyheim/internet4cats.html to read my FAQ on "Cats from Outer Space."

You Can Also Get Cat FAQs via E-mail

If you don't have access to the Web, you can get FAQs by e-mail. On the following pages are nearly two dozen FAQs you can request. To get the FAQ that you want, send an e-mail message to **mail-server@rtfm.mit.edu.** Leave the subject line of the message blank, or just type a period if you must type something. In the body of the message, type the boldfaced command from the following pages that pertains to the FAQ you want, then send your message. So, for example, to get the guide to the cat FAQs type **send usenet/news. answers/cats-faq/table-of-contents** in the body of your message.

In response, the computer will send you an e-mail message with the FAQ that you requested. The only FAQs you can obtain this way are the ones assembled from information circulated in the Usenet newsgroup rec.pets.cats. You'll need to use other means to obtain some of the more specialized cat breed FAQs described elsewhere in this chapter.

send usenet/news.answers/cats-faq/table-of-contents   The guide to the cat FAQs.

send usenet/news.answers/cats-faq/getting-a-cat   What every cat should know before letting a human move in.

send usenet/news.answers/cats-faq/general-care   How your human should take care of you.

send usenet/news.answers/cats-faq/health-care   Cat health-care advice.

send usenet/news.answers/cats-faq/medical-info   More cat health-care advice.

send usenet/news.answers/cats-faq/outside-world   Cats and the outside world.

send usenet/news.answers/cats-faq/behavior   "Cures" for supposed cat behavioral problems.

send usenet/news.answers/cats-faq/leukemia   Feline leukemia.

send usenet/news.answers/cats-faq/misc   Miscellaneous issues, like purring, catnip, allergies, and pregnant women and cats.

send usenet/news.answers/cats-faq/resources
Recommended cat books and Internet resources for cats.

send usenet/news.answers/cats-faq/breeds/ bombays   Bombay cats.

send usenet/news.answers/cats-faq/breeds/ chartreux   Chartreux cats.

send usenet/news.answers/cats-faq/breeds/ coons   Maine coon cats.

send usenet/news.answers/cats-faq/breeds/ korats   Korat cats.

send usenet/news.answers/cats-faq/breeds/ ragdolls   Ragdoll cats.

send usenet/news.answers/cats-faq/breeds/ somalis   Somali cats.

send usenet/news.answers/cats-faq/ trad-siamese   Siamese cats.

send usenet/news.answers/pets/pet-loss
Pet loss.

send usenet/news.answers/pets/fleas-ticks
How to get rid of fleas.

Cat Net Surfer Tip

It's OK to fantasize about catching a gopher server and leaving its carcass on the neighbor's deck. Just make sure that no one's around to laugh at you when you start batting at the computer screen.

178

You Can Also Get Cat FAQs via FTP

You can get any of the FAQs listed on pp. 178–179 by FTP (file transfer protocol). FTP is a way of telling a faraway computer to send you a file. To use FTP, begin by typing an FTP address into your Internet software. That address might look something like ftp.catstuff.com. When you press ENTER or choose OK (depending on your software), your computer goes in search of that FTP location, more commonly called a site. Once it finds the right site, you can browse the files on the distant computer and download any that interest you.

To download the cat FAQs using FTP, send your Internet FTP software to **rtfm.mit.edu**. If you've got a direct Internet connection (through a service like Netcom), you'll need to locate the FTP option and then type **ftp.rtfm.mit.edu**. If you access the Internet through CompuServe, America Online, or Prodigy, choose FTP from the main Internet menu, then type in the address **rtfm.mit.edu** (you probably won't need to type **ftp** before the address).

When you reach the site, you'll probably receive a message asking for your name. This message is coming from the computer that you've just dialed into. Type or choose the word **anonymous** in response to this question. Next you'll be asked for your password; type in your full Internet address.

Once you've connected to the FTP site at MIT, go to the directory of cat FAQs by typing **cd usenet/news.answers/cats-faq** or **usenet/news.answers/pets**. Once in the proper directory, type **get *filenameyouwant***, using the list of FAQ files on pp. 178–179. For example, if you want the FAQ on getting a cat you would type **get getting-a-cat**; for the pet loss FAQ you would type **get pet-loss**, and so on. Press ENTER once you've finished typing your request for the file.

Cat Net Surfer Tip

When you jump on the monitor, always land in the center. Otherwise it may tip over backwards and knock you off.

181

Advanced Keyboard Trick
CREATE KEYBOARD MACROS
WITH YOUR TAIL

Using a computer can be frustrating. Perhaps never more so than when you're patiently watching the floppy drive door, waiting for a mouse to emerge (you swear you saw one run in), and your human refuses to watch with you. He continues blithely tapping away at his inane budgeting program while you do all the work. What to do? Simple. Program a keyboard macro—with your tail!

Start by swishing your tail side to side over the keyboard and chattering excitedly. When your human pushes your tail aside, smack it back. Eventually you'll annoy him enough so that he'll try to remove you from the desk. Now you need to think fast. Grab the top of the monitor with your front paws and kick your back feet. Meanwhile, pound your tail against the keyboard. As your human struggles to pull you from the desk, wriggle harder.

When the wrestling match is over, you'll have not only created a new set of macros but, if you were clever enough, also renamed hard drives, created a new boot-up sequence, and even given your human new CMOS settings in his computer's BIOS.

Appendix

MORE FROM CAT

CYBERSPACE

THE RAINBOW BRIDGE

The passing of a beloved cat is understandably traumatic for most humans. Gone forever are their carefree days of opening cat-food cans and running masking tape over the furniture in a hopeless attempt to remove the cat hair before their guests arrive. Without us, they're innocents adrift in a wicked world, easy prey for anyone who wants to convince them to adopt a dog.

If you're part of a multi-cat household that has experienced a loss, or if you simply want to prepare your human for the inevitable, look into online pet-loss support groups. Those on America Online and CompuServe even provide compassionate online counselors. The Internet cat mailing lists Feline-L and Cats-L are also good places to find a shoulder to sob on.

Many humans suffering the loss of their cat find solace in a poem about the animal hereafter called "The Legend of Rainbow Bridge." It has even inspired a candle-lighting ceremony that animal lovers across the online services participate in. Names of sick and deceased pets are collected via e-mail each week, then posted on the services. At a designated time, participants light candles and recite a prayer in memory of the animals.

"Rainbow Bridge" is one of the most frequently requested files on the Internet; several versions are in circulation. The original author is unknown. Here's my own rendition with a bit of commentary.

The Legend of Rainbow Bridge

Between heaven and earth is a bridge called Rainbow Bridge. On the side near earth is a land of fragrant meadows and verdant prairies. When an animal who was loved on earth dies, he goes to this Eden-like land.

His youth is restored, his infirmities healed. His eyes are made bright and his fur shines. He forgets that he was ever in pain. He forgets what sickness and hunger are about. All day long, he runs through the meadows, cavorting with other animals, playing the games he loved on earth. But something is missing. He remembers this whenever he leaps for a ball, like in the old days, or rests in the cool grass and finds himself listening for familiar footsteps. He remembers: He is not with the person he loved on earth. That's why his heart aches.

Then one day when he is playing, he recognizes a figure in the distance. He stops to look. His heart beats hard. His nose instinctively sniffs the air. Suddenly, he runs from the group. His legs propel him over the ground toward you.

You fall upon each other and embrace. His face nestles yours, and your arms wrap around him. He licks your cheek and you stroke his ears and hold him close like in the old days. You both cross the bridge together, never to be separated again.

Bubbles the Cat's Commentary: You and I know that this whole scenario is absurd. When we cats die, we don't hang around some creaky bridge with a bunch of dead dogs. We move into luxury beach-front condos with track lighting and climate control. We are given our choice of Art Deco, Bauhaus, French Provincial, or Ralph Lauren furniture (although most of us simply prefer carpet-covered cat trees). Best of all, there's no one lurking in the shadows with a squirt gun, prepared to aim it at us whenever we hop on the Queen Anne desk.

In spite of what the poem says, we do not play with other animals, especially not with all the dead gerbils lying around. Instead, we watch a lot of TV. (*Nova* nature documentaries are favorites). At night we get together and pig out on gefilte fish stuffed with marshmallows. Sometimes we band together into a wild cat pack and head out to Rainbow Bridge to scare the bejeebers out of the dead parakeets.

When our humans eventually join us, we don't go capering over mushy fields to greet them. We stand in the doorway, aloof, amazed that they made it into heaven, peeved that it took them so long. Unless of course we happen to be hungry and they happen to be carrying a can opener. Unfortunately, most humans don't die with can openers in their hands.

INTERNET CAT CODES

Cat lovers on the Internet have developed a short-hand to describe their cats. They dutifully type these codes after their own names at the end of every e-mail message they write. For instance, a lap-sized Cornish Rex named Ursula with blue eyes, a healthy appetite, and a mind of her own would be signified this way:

Ursula: CR B 6 X L W+ I+++ T—- A+++ E+++ H S+ V F- Q++ P B PA PL++

Here is a complete list of the cat codes, as maintained by Eric Williams, an Internet cat lover. (For an up-to-date version see his cat code page at **http://turnpike.net/metro/sapphyr/catcode. html**.)

Cat's Name

Type the cat's name—either its familiar name or its formal pedigree name—followed by a colon. For example: **Snuffy:** or **Dream-Maker's Lady Vesuvius Latitia Del Carrero Bechamel "Snuffy":**

Appearance

After the cat's name, list the following abbreviations to describe its physical attributes. Breed codes come first, followed by fur color and pattern codes, then codes to describe eyes, age, sex, size, and so on.

Breed Codes

If your cat is a mixed breed and you know the breeds, list their codes after the cat's name in descending order of predominance. For example, **Elmo: NF+NB** designates a cat that is largely Norwegian Forest and to a lesser degree Nebelung.

If you are unsure of your cat's breed but your cat resembles one or more breeds, you may designate this by enclosing the breed codes in quotation marks. For instance, **Davis: "SX"** designates a cat that may or may not be a Sphynx but certainly looks like one.

AB	Abyssinian	**JB**	Japanese Bobtail
AC	American Curl	**KT**	Korat
AL	American Longhair	**MC**	Maine Coon
AS	American Shorthair	**MX**	Manx
AW	American Wirehair	**NB**	Nebelung
BA	Balinese	**NF**	Norwegian Forest
BB	American Bobtail	**OC**	Ocicat
BG	Bengal	**OL**	Oriental Longhair
BI	Birman	**OS**	Oriental Shorthair
BO	Bombay	**PS**	Persian
BR	Bristol	**RB**	Russian Blue
BS	British Shorthair	**RD**	Ragdoll
BU	Burmese	**SA**	Safari
CR	Cornish Rex	**SF**	Scottish Fold
CX	Chartreux	**SG**	Singapura
CY	Cymric	**SI**	Siamese

DL	Domestic Longhair	**SN**	Snowshoe
DM	Domestic Mediumhair	**SO**	Somali
DR	Devon Rex	**SP**	California Spangled
DS	Domestic Shorthair	**SR**	Selkirk Rex
EM	Egyptian Mau	**SS**	Scottish Fold Longhair
ES	Exotic Shorthair	**SX**	Sphynx
EU	European Shorthair	**TA**	Turkish Angora
GR	German Rex	**TF**	Tiffany
HB	Havana Brown	**TO**	Tonkinese
HI	Himalayan	**TV**	Turkish Van
JA	Javanese		

Fur Color

You may combine fur color codes to designate mixed-color cats. List the colors in order of predominance. For instance, a black cat with white paws might be designated like this: **Toby: B+W**.

B	Black
C	Chocolate
D	Ruddy
G	Gold
L	Lilac
O	Brown
R	Red (also sometimes called orange)
S	Silver
W	White

Fur Pattern

Use these codes as modifiers to the fur color codes to describe the patterning of your cat's fur. You may add these modifiers to individual color codes or to combinations of codes (for example, **W+Bd** would translate "white cat with gray patches"). You may also apply these modifiers to groups of colors by using parentheses. For instance, **(W+B+R)d** would signify a cat that is predominantly white with diluted black and red coloring as well—in other words, a calico. **(R+W)t+W** would designate a cat that has mostly red-and-white tabby markings but a few white spots, too.

c	Chinchilla
d	Diluted (in other words, black fur fades into gray in spots; red or orange fades into cream)
h	Shaded
k	Ticked
m	Mink
o	Spotted
p	Pointed
r	Tortoiseshell
s	Smoke
t	Tabby (can be either classic or mackerel patterns)
v	Van

Eye Color

If your cat's eyes don't fit neatly into any of the color categories below, you may signify a color mix with a plus sign. For instance, hazel-gold eyes would be represented as **H+Y**. If your cat has different colored eyes, you may list both colors with a slash. For example: **B/G**.

A   Aqua

B   Blue

C   Copper

G   Green

H   Hazel

Y   Gold (also known as yellow)

Age

A cat's age is specified in years.months format. For instance, a cat that is five years old would be designated **5**; a cat that is 17 months, **1.5**; and a cat that is three months old, **.3**.

Sex

Many cats consider their sexuality a private matter and would not appreciate it if you broadcast details of their sex lives across the Internet each time you sent an e-mail message. Before appending one of these cat codes to your cat's name, please discuss the matter with your cat:

X   Female, spayed, no interest.

X+   Female, spayed, but still interested.

X++   Female, intact, but not particularly excitable.

X+++   I am a kitten factory.

Y   Male, neutered, no interest.

Y+   Male, neutered, but still interested.

Y++   Male, intact, but not particularly excitable.

Y+++   I would climb a burning cat tree to get to a female in heat.

Size

L−−−   I can fit into a shirt pocket.

L−−   I can curl up in two cupped hands.

L−   I'm between kitten-size and adult-size.

L   I'm an average cat, just right for your lap.

L+   I'm starting to slip off laps.

L++   I'm big enough to instill fear in a German shepherd.

L+++   People mistake me for a mountain lion.

Weight

W‑‑   So thin you can count my bones.

W‑   Slim, but healthy.

W   Average build, not too thin, not too fat.

W+   Yeah, I'm big, but it's all muscle.

W++   Crack open the Nutra-Slim.

Claws

C‑‑‑   Fully declawed.

C‑‑   Declawed only in the front.

C‑   My claws are protected with Soft Paws.

C+   My claws are clipped regularly.

C++   I don't like pedicures, but my claws are dull.

C+++   I have ten razor-sharp implements of death.

Note: Add an asterisk to your cat's claw code to signify that it has extra claws.

Behavior

Codes that signify behavioral traits are optional. If your cat is normal in any category (whatever that means), you may omit the corresponding code in order to keep your cat codes to a manageable length.

Indoor/Outdoor Preferences

I–––   Why would anyone want to live in a stuffy house?

I––   I'm allowed inside once in a while, but I eat and sleep outdoors.

I–   I come indoors to sleep and eat, but not much else.

I   I drift between indoor and outdoor life.

I+   I prefer to live indoors but go outside when I feel like it.

I++   I live indoors most of the time, but I sneak out sometimes.

I+++   You mean there's a world outside the house?

Temperament

T–––   Don't touch me or I'll shred you!

T––   I'm annoyed by human contact and avoid it.

T–   People are OK for begging food from and playing with, but not much else.

T   I have a few special humans I like; the rest I tolerate.

T+   I'm shy about meeting new people but affectionate with those I know.

T++   I like meeting new people and am affectionate with most.

T+++   I'm a cuddly ball of affection and I love everybody.

Note: You may designate a split personality with a combination of pluses and minuses separated by a slash. For instance, a cat that is sometimes annoyed by human contact but sometimes enjoys meeting new people would be designated thus: T––/++.

Energy Level

A––– They think I'm dead until they start the can opener.

A–– I may show signs of life in the presence of an excellent toy.

A– I work hard at sleeping, but I like to chase an occasional fly.

A I like to play, but I like sleep too.

A+ If you don't play with me, I'll find a way to play by myself.

A++ I'm always getting into things.

A+++ All photos of me are blurred.

Eating Habits

E––– I eat just enough to get by.

E–– I'd rather play with a toy than eat.

E– I'll wait until the other cats have eaten before I eat.

E I enjoy good food, but sometimes the stuff I get is fit for a litter box.

E+ I would rather eat than play.

E++ The kitchen is my favorite hangout.

E+++ Nothing even remotely edible is safe when I'm around.

Hunting Tendencies

H I would never think of eating anything that didn't come in a can.

H+ I chase anything that moves, but if I catch it I don't know what to do with it.

H++ I bag an occasional rodent but rarely eat it.

H+++ I'm a skilled hunter and keep myself fed, but I like humans to feed me too.

H++++ If I didn't kill it, I don't want it on my plate.

Smurgling

Smurgling is the act of kneading some part of a human's body or clothing while simultaneously nuzzling, licking, or sucking.

S   I'd use nonclumping cat litter before I'd smurgle.

S+   I sneak an occasional smurgle.

S++   When I'm in the mood, I smurgle with the best of them.

S+++   Everybody leaves my house moistened with kitty drool.

Vocalization

V---   If you toss me off the computer monitor, I may squeak a protest.

V--   I know how to meow to social equals but have yet to meet one.

V-   I sometimes meow for food but must be especially hungry to do so.

V   I'll certainly let you know when it's dinner time, but don't expect to hear from me until then.

V+   I have a small but useful vocabulary of important meows signifying *food*, *play*, and *clean the box.*

V++   I have long, meaningful conversations with people.

V+++   Everyone in the neighborhood deserves to hear my magnificent voice.

Fetching

F–   Why did you throw that thing?

F   I'll chase it if you throw it, but don't expect me to bring it back.

F+   I can be coaxed into fetching a favorite object when I'm in the mood.

F++   I like to fetch and will often ask my human to throw things for me.

F+++   I fetch as enthusiastically as a dog (but better, of course).

Intelligence

Q– – –   Every time I blink, I discover a whole new world.

Q– –   Complex principles, like gravity, escape me.

Q–   I'm slow, but I'm trying.

Q   I'm an average cat, with cunning but no real reasoning ability.

Q+   I'm pretty quick-witted for a cat.

Q++   I display near-human reasoning sometimes.

Q+++   I'm working on my Ph.D. thesis.

Lap Affinity

P–   I'd rather lie on concrete than in a lap.

P   I'll sit on a lap if I'm in the mood.

P+   I prefer laps to any other resting place, but they must belong to people I like.

P++   I'm a total lap fungus.

Belly Sensitivity

B--   Touch my belly, and I'll take your arm off.

B-   I like to lie on my back and sun my belly, but don't you touch it.

B   I like my belly rubbed, but not too much.

B+   Please rub my belly!

B++   I like to have my belly drummed.

Purr Enthusiasm

PA--   Me, purr?

PA-   I'll think about it if you pet me enough.

PA   I like to show my appreciation whenever I'm petted or fed.

PA+   Pet me, and I immediately rumble.

PA++   I purr as soon as my favorite human enters the room.

Purr Volume

PL---   You might feel me vibrate, but you probably won't hear me.

PL--   You need to put your ear against my tummy to hear me.

PL-   On the quiet side.

PL   Average volume.

PL+   Louder than the average cat.

PL++   A power purrer!

PL+++   I've been known to set off car alarms.

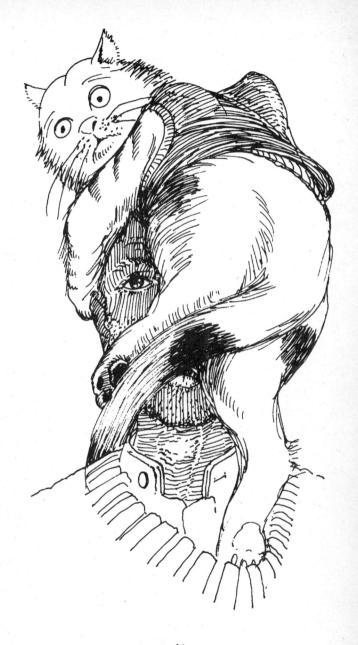

RECOMMENDED READING

***Internet for Cats & Dummies* by Victor Les Chats**—The latest installment in the popular Dummies series of computer books. This one focuses on how to tell if you've started a flame war on the Internet and, if so, how to escape blame and bodily harm. An appendix offers advice for those of us who've been banished for life from Usenet discussion groups like rec.pets.dogs.

***E-mail Addresses of Rich & Powerful Cats* by Kiko Katmandu**—A whole bunch of e-mail addresses for cats you'd like to meet. Unfortunately none of the cats listed ever answer their e-mail because they are not convinced that they would derive any personal benefit from doing so.

***Gopher and WAIS: How Edible Are They?* by Tabitha Furfactory**—A well-researched investigation into the question foremost in every cat's mind: If I eat a gopher server, how long will it be before I spit it up behind the computer?

***Cybercat!* by Andre Caterwaul**—Follow the adventures of a mild-mannered tabby as he assumes 157 e-mail aliases to terrorize canine denizens of the popular Internet mailing list for dogs, Rottie-L. In the sequel, *Cybercat II: Hell Revisited*, he goes undercover again, this time to expose the activities in the mailing list for scent hounds, Nose-L.

***The Internet Yellow Pages for Cats* by Theolonius Whiskerfolk**—Really a directory of Internet places you don't want to visit. This exhaustive guide puts at your fingertips compelling reasons for sneering at any Internet database or discussion group you might tap into. For instance, under Complete Text of Descartes' Discourse on Reason, the guide advises: "You're a cat. You have your own reason. Why do you need someone else's?" Under Symbolic Algebra Usenet Newsgroup, you'll be told, "You have six toes on each foot. Algebra was created by someone with five toes. Could anything be less relevant to your life?"

***Internet Cat Paths* by Bebe Cattywampus** — You know what cat paths are in a garden (they're the trails cats walk daily to survey their kingdoms), but do you know how to use them on the Internet? This hands-on tutorial will show you step-by-step how to stake out your own personal cat paths in cyberspace and how to defend them from nefarious intruders like computer scientists, mathematicians, ground squirrels, and voles.